Would You Work for You?

The Quest: Discovering the Leader Within

Chris J. Ihrig
Dr. Timothy Yeomans

Fired Up Publishing, Inc.
Puyallup, WA

This edition published by Fired Up Publishing, a division of Fired Up Brands, Inc. For information contact Fired Up Brands, Puyallup, WA.

First Edition
ISBN 978-1-7366624-0-3
Cataloging-in-Publication Data

Ihrig, Chris J., 1967-
Yeomans, Timothy, 1964 -
Would You Work for You – The Quest: Discovering the Leader Within / Chris J. Ihrig & Dr. Timothy Yeomans. -- 1st ed.p. cm.

Includes bibliographical references and index.

Summary: "Describes the initial step for of a process for developing a leadership map for inspiring others,
building great teams, achieving breakthrough results, and transforming a business culture."--Provided by publisher.

ISBN 978-1-7366624-0-3 (pbk. : alk. paper)
1. Leadership. 2. Organizational behavior. 3. Organizational
effectiveness. 4. Management--Employee participation. 5. Responsibility.
6. Self-management 7. Workplace Culture.

Editing and Proofing by Matthew Ralph
Exterior cover design by Vanessa Mendozzi
Interior book design by Probookdesigns

Manufactured in the United States of America

To our wonderful families and friends.

Being with you brings us tremendous joy and encouragement. Along each step of the journey, you have remained steady and positive voices. We have grown because of you. It is with deep appreciation and love that we share this body of work as a small token of thanks for speaking into our lives and believing in us.

- Chris & Tim

TABLE OF CONTENTS

INTRODUCTION

My name is Chris Ihrig and I'm CEO and Founder of Fired Up Culture, a leadership coaching and workplace culture consulting firm. I have written this book with my longtime friend and colleague, Tim Yeomans. We refer to ourselves as "Coach Chris" and "Coach Tim" throughout. The two of us represent a growing team of talented professionals at Fired Up Culture. We get up each day driven by the purpose of equipping leaders.

When we began to work on this project, we envisioned one book with multiple key sections based on the models we use at Fired Up Culture. At the core of our model is a framework to assist leadership to activate a set of principles and practices to drive change in their organizations. The four-step framework, Lead Self, Lead Others, Lead Team, and Lead Your Culture, is simple in theory but not always easy to execute.

Our work has taken us around the globe and afforded us the opportunity to partner with leaders who are guiding diverse organizations. Some of these organizations are small and local, while others are large and global. Whether a not-for-profit or a publicly held company, one thing is true: leadership matters. Our team has made it our mission to work alongside leaders, equip them to become champions of workplace culture, and be the change agents our world needs.

A few years ago, I stood in front of a packed ballroom of CEOs. As Founder and CEO of a growing and dynamic workplace culture consulting firm, I was sharing a few thoughts on a topic that had been keeping me up at night. It was simple, but for me, a profound and life-changing question: **"Would you work for you?"**

During the presentation, I was sharing many of the important factors necessary to move an organization into a space of increased productivity. The conversation dealing with the importance of building trust and teamwork while creating an attractive "employment brand" was being explored at length. However, something magical happened when this question popped up on the screen behind me: "Would you work for you?"

This question prompted a visible response from the faces I was looking at. They leaned forward, people grabbed the pen and paper sitting in front of them and phones went up to snap a picture of the screen. I knew at that moment that the conversation was going to be different.

The response from the audience during the presentation and the extensive conversations that followed with many of the CEOs in attendance demonstrated the power and resonance of the question. This one question prompted so many other questions in their minds. Questions such as: does the company or organization that I lead support and live by the values that will attract and retain top talent? Am I, as a leader, creating and nurturing a culture where success and productivity are sustained? Is the workplace aligned with our missions, visions, and goals? Am I the leader I would want to work for?

For me, the power of the question "Would you work for you?" was not only personally jarring but it also eloquently summarized what the core purpose of the lifelong work I'd been doing over the last several decades. This question, "Would you work for you?" had become the enhanced vision and mission for our work.

In our consultations with successful businesses and non-profit organizations seeking to take the "next step" in building their brand and culture, we have become even more aware of how this conversation, at the highest levels of business, was causing leaders to reflect upon and rethink long-held business and corporate culture practices. Is what we're doing today, and replicating month over month, moving us forward in alignment with our stated values and corporate goals? Are we creating a place we would want to work?

What began as a presentation quickly transitioned into a personal and professional journey. The pages that follow have been crafted in response to the many questions and conversations that have followed with CEOs since that presentation. Being a leader that can drive results for the long term, in a context where managers, team members, and support staff feel genuinely part of the team, is a skill that can be learned and enhanced.

Helping those who work towards our common goal (to feel vital to the success of the company) requires an intentional focus. Creating an organizational culture, where belonging and identification with the brand are as strong internally as externally, is a place from which long-term success can be derived.

So, it is here we present the first step in this journey which is simply referred to as "The Quest". It's a journey of effectively leading self. A journey of growth and the never-ending pursuit of self-development. We quickly realized that one large book was not going to be the best vehicle for exploring this topic. And with a quick pivot, we broke the original book concept into a four-part leadership journey.

Together, Tim and I have continued to spend many hours of conversation around this one thought-provoking question and the impact it's having on our work. More importantly, the transformation that the conversation is having within us as leaders. Imagine the potential growth and productivity when the answer to the question of "Would you work for you?" is an unequivocal "YES!"

You may currently hold the title of CEO and consider yourself an experienced, seasoned and wisdom-filled veteran. Alternatively, you may be aspiring to lead at this level in the future. Whatever professional chair you find yourself sitting in today, the pages you're about to read were written for you. We invite you to the conversation. We invite you to come on this journey with us.

The question of "Would you work for you"? begins with awareness of the expectations of leadership and how you can work to lead yourself, others, teams, and eventually create culture!

We invite you to join us on the quest. More importantly, we look forward to connecting our story with yours and hearing of the impact your leadership is having on your world.

Coach Chris & Coach Tim

Coaching Corner (Coach Chris & Coach Tim)

Throughout the book you will notice some call out boxes we call the "Coaching Corner". Written by Tim or Chris or both, the Coaching Corner is intended to give you a specific action to take.

We encourage you to put your leadership into action by taking the recommended steps and access the highlighted resource. Before diving too deep into the concepts of this book in the *Would You Work for You Series*, we want to encourage you to use the link below to take a complimentary assessment of where you stand as a leader. This assessment will take you about 7 minutes to complete. Not a huge time investment by any standard, but what it will do for you is provide a guide. A guide to the areas that you potentially could focus in on as you undertake this quest for leadership.

Take Your Complimentary Leadership Assessment by visiting www.wouldyouworkforyou.com/resources

CHAPTER 1:
Why Not You?

"Always be a first-rate version of yourself and not a second-rate version of someone else."

– Judy Garland

Throhe fact that you've picked up this book and began reading sets you apart. You've placed yourself into a club. This is not a secret club, mind you, but one that lots of people have been invited to but they ultimately decided to turn down the invitation. There are also others who gave it a trial run and simply discovered it was hard work and chose a different route.

"The club" is leadership; it's a calling and you've decided to take your first steps on the journey toward discovering your leadership style — or your "voice" as we like to call it. And from our vantage point as coaches, we see it as undertaking a quest. This quest will push you to reflect and learn, and there will, of course, be moments of frustration and doubt. But here is what we do know. After working with thousands of people and countless hours of coaching leaders along the way, people that plan and persevere usually end up having a highly rewarding experience. This kind of experience will have a significant impact on you, both personally and professionally. So, we simply ask: why not you?

Everybody influences somebody. All of us are leaders in some areas of our lives, and followers in others. This is true whether you have titles or clearly defined roles, or not. It is also true that we never know who, or how much, we influence those around us.

In our society, people often perpetuate the myth that leaders are born, not made. While it's true that some traits, such as a strong personality and being a quick thinker, are often associated with being a leader, it does not mean they prepare someone to actually *be* a leader. Modern society is quick to confuse the roles and obligations of leadership with positional authority and titles. As we like to say, *"Being a leader does not require a title and having a title does not make you one either."*

The quest for leadership is not about luck or chance. Being a leader is a choice. It's a choice to prepare yourself to serve and support the people around you. It's a choice to embrace challenges and see difficult tasks through to a positive conclusion. It means failing from time to time as well as learning from and accepting responsibility for your own mistakes.

Being a leader means that you fundamentally understand the power and impact of positive relationships. The point of leadership is to recognize and facilitate systems to help make the work of team members meaningful and efficient. Great leaders also embrace the challenge and the duty of making those around them better in every respect.

The choice to embark on the journey of leadership is about so much more than simply securing a promotion or receiving a new title. It's a commitment to constant self-reflection and self-improvement. It's about acquiring a deep understanding of how people and teams work together, as well as building teams and growing their collective capacity to succeed. The quest for leadership must start with the understanding that leadership is not a title; it's more about the attitude of service through influence.

With this increased influence comes additional responsibilities, expectations, and accountabilities. Leadership often requires extra effort and time to create solutions to difficult questions and support the mission and purpose of the organization. The role of a leader implies creating a culture and framework to get the best work out of employees, quickly and easily.

Choosing to prepare for the privilege of leadership means having an understanding that your actions and decisions will have an impact on the lives of many. For any actions and decisions to have a positive impact, you need to be willing to prepare and lead.

Your development as a leader is serious business. But make sure you let yourself have fun as you take this journey. This is a chance to learn about yourself, grow as a leader, and build an amazing life. Approach it with intent but a light-hearted spirit and an open mind. That'll take you far and the rewards will be abundant. But we also encourage you to not try and hold a tight rein on the path you're about to take. Most great adventures work that way. You don't plan them and you don't wait to get all the details right – you just do them.

> *"Great leaders don't set out to be a leader, they set out to make a difference. It's never about the role, always about the goal."*
> *– Jeremy Bravo*

The Roadmap to Leadership Success

The beginning of the quest for leadership and the process of "leading self" involve great deal of attention to master skills and habits that will underpin success. It's like a map. If you forget or are missing an important part of the map and end up taking a wrong turn, there will be issues. The art and science of being a leader is no different. There is a map that works.

Throughout this book, we're here to assist you in creating and mastering your own map. But before placing all those pieces on the table for discussion, I want to be clear about one important concept:

At its very core, leadership is about relationships.

When you become a leader, being *prepared* to lead would seem self-evident. Yet, if we examine the above statement more deeply, it will become clear that people with highly developed skills and habits will stand a much better chance of success. Great leaders work at it. We refer to this as your capacity for 'relational success'. Those who fundamentally understand the importance and value of positive working relationships, in addition to supportive systems, and building the capacity of team members at all levels, will flourish where others will struggle.

Your successful career as a leader will be defined by the quality of the relationships you build and they will become the cornerstone of your career. Striving to be the most thoughtful, aware, and generous person within an organization is a good place to begin. The expertise and abilities that allow you to guide others, teams, and whole organizations, will be critical without question.

Most successful leaders have mastered the skills needed to transcend the *transactional space*, i.e., tasks, to-do lists and actions. They then intentionally move into the *transformational space*, i.e., using transactions to drive impact, add value and make change happen. This is done through models of improvement, development and growth that positively impacts the relationships around them. Serving others while leading an enterprise will require expertise in all of the aforementioned areas: relationships, systems, and capacity building.

Creating an atmosphere of "we" rather than "me" will be an experience that you'll be thanked for in the future. Using your newly found skills for the betterment of others, in addition to your own success, will make your journey and the final destination much more gratifying.

Learning (and Owning) Your Craft

One of the key aspects of growing into your leadership role, both your current one and the ones that will be in your future, is to bring value. Frankly, if you don't bring value to your work (value that actually solves business issues and drives business results), it's likely you won't be offered many leadership opportunities.

Deeply understanding the business or craft that you will eventually lead, is a strong place to begin your leadership journey from. Bringing such important expertise to the table can place you in a position, early on, to be a "value-added" person on a team. Expertise provides a leader with a great deal of credibility with regard to the technical aspects of the role.

What we know from years of research is that technical ability alone, while very helpful, will not alone bring about the positive changes in the productivity of a team. Without the understanding of how leadership can serve as a catalyst to that process, technical ability alone will provide only the partial preparation required for a successful leadership role. In addition to this, a foundational understanding of how organizations function and how the team members can be supported, to maximize their contributions, will be necessary for the team to achieve at the highest level.

> *"Hope is wishing something would happen. Faith is believing something will happen. Courage is making something happen." – Unknown*

As an aspiring leader, having the ability to see the challenges from the perspective of all members of the team provides a great advantage. To be able to connect with team members in their realm of expertise requires an investment of time and energy. You need to actively listen and learn about the different facets of their roles and add that to your own base of knowledge. Knowing what support a leader can bring to a member of the team, and what will make them the most productive in their role, highlights the leadership quality of service. In this case, that means service to others.

Anticipating the needs of fellow team members can be as simple as making certain that the necessary supplies are always available. It can also be rooted in the understanding of how time and schedules between team members intersect, and where the inherent conflict of those schedules is likely to cause difficulty.

The beginnings of effective leadership can be found in people who are intentionally "tuned in" to the needs of those around them. They take proactive steps to ensure that whatever is required for that team to function at a high level, is in place.

It turns out that becoming a leader, and doing something amazing with your life, hinges on what makes you different, not on what makes you the same as everyone else. Don't try to replicate what you see in others. Instead, make your own music and write your own script. Own who you are and craft your leadership in a way that fully aligns with your own unique voice and the person you desire to be in this world.

Coaching Corner (Coach Chris)

I love a good map. I was trying to explain to my 19-year-old that in the past, you didn't have the option of looking something up on your phone and have a GPS voice tell you that the route is being recalculated when you take a wrong turn. My son looked a little confused when I said that maps used to be made of paper and sit in your car's glovebox.

Here are a few coaching tips for making the leadership map your own:

Start with what you know. Journeys always start from where you are. Begin with the foundational pieces that exist in all great leaders: self-awareness, values, character, vision and communication style.

Make it your own. Once you feel comfortable with the basic map for leadership, make it your own. Tap into your own beliefs, values, strengths, and creativity and bring your unique leadership voice to life.

Craft your Brand. Create your own leadership brand that exudes your personality and passion.

> *"Do not wait; the time will never be 'just right.' Start where you stand, and work with whatever tools you may have at your command, and better tools will be found as you go along." – George Herbert*

The Leadership Mindset

Our mindset as a leader is critical. The perceptions that we hold will either enhance or impede our journey toward success. Our mindset and the perceptions we create are significant in how we make sense of the world around us. Most of us tend to have a "fixed mindset" in this regard. Having a "growth mindset" demonstrates an openness to learning and a willingness to see the possible, rather than the barriers present in a given situation. Just the mere act of picking up this book and investing in yourself demonstrates your growth mindset.

Having frameworks for processing your thoughts and actions will allow you to more easily tackle the challenges that come your way. Your success will be dependent on your ability to mentally reframe present and past experiences and shape the thoughts for the most positive outcomes possible. Carol Dweck in her book *Mindset* speaks about the growth mindset and the positive impacts that such an outlook can have as you lead yourself.

It's a myth that talent alone is the only thing necessary for high levels of accomplishment. As we've studied and observed successful leaders over the years, we've noticed a pattern of perseverance that allowed these men and women to navigate through challenging places in their journeys. Their perseverance often comes down to their willingness to embrace and live out a growth mindset.

A growth mindset is more than just being optimistic. It involves a belief in yourself and others, while always striving to bring out true potential. It involves the capacity to move on from disappointment and failure, through a lens of learning and growing from the experience. It also shows that such experiences, even the painful ones, can be applied (in a positive way) in the future to achieve the larger goals you aspire to.

As you dive deeper into the *Would You Work for You* series, you'll notice common themes throughout. At the core, we will continue to explore how relationships, especially those we hold most dear, are heavily impacted by the way we choose to frame them in our minds. Our mindset has a direct application to happiness, future growth, our success and the impact on our relationships as leaders.

Coaching Corner (Coach Tim)

Shawn Achor, author of the book *The Happiness Advantage*, speaks directly to how our perception of the world and our current situation can greatly affect our future success.

We've all heard the old adage that "attitude is everything". Achor explains how the daily act of sending at least three positive messages to colleagues helps us to see the good in others. Taking time to journal about the positive aspects of our lives helps us focus on what is possible.

Anchor shares that making time for daily exercise teaches us that our actions have a direct result on our well-being. Creating a positive perception of our workplace environment can also greatly enhance our personal satisfaction while working. Taking time to reflect and affirm the work of those around us allows us to actively appreciate the contributions of others. It also allows us to reflect on how we can help them to be better in their work as well.

Invest in You!

Growing into the leader you see yourself becoming starts with how you choose to invest in you. The way you lead yourself and care for yourself will be witnessed by others. The investments you make will translate into deeper self-confidence and connection.

In order to make the right investments, your quest must focus on what makes you unique. Get to know yourself. Be kind and caring to yourself. Remember; most of us behave and perform well when things are 'humming along'. But our behaviors change quite a lot when challenging times arrive. Stress does funny things to our attitudes and it affects how we act and treat those around us. None of us are immune to stress, but how you handle it will differentiate you from many other people.

The time to make investments, grow and establish who you're going to be as a leader, happens during times of calm and predictability. Invest in yourself before things become too big, out of hand or stressful.

Be excited about your dreams, ideas, and future. Make the investments today and take the steps needed to move you toward your goals. You can, and will, be a great leader.

> *"If you do not know where you are going... then any road will take you there."* – *Lewis Carrol*

Coaching Corner (Coach Tim)

- Start small
- Start early
- Start now

Take a moment to review your life. Identify five areas where you lack discipline and you'd like to see improved. Put them in order of priority that you want to work on. Start tackling them one at a time but stick to one and focus on it for 60 days before you move to the next. As you progress, don't forget to celebrate the progress along the way.

Are You Willing to Pay the Price?

In case you haven't already noticed, leadership is a completely crazy way to choose to spend your life. But it's also ridiculously amazing. When you can maximize your potential as a leader, the positive impact you will have on others is endless and the rewards are top notch.

What do you want? What does it cost? Are you willing to make the commitment and pay the price? So many questions, so little time.

Your leadership quest has a starting point. Like a good vacation, the planning takes work but deciding where you're wanting to go is critical. The vision and the view of the journey you want to take will make it clear what things you need to pack and how to best prepare for what is in store.

As you prepare for the initial steps of leading yourself, the responsibly of leading others is best met through intentional and thoughtful preparation. Lou Holtz, a famous American football coach, once quipped, *"We don't want to be on the hope and wonder program... hoping this works and wondering why it didn't."*

As you undertake the leadership quest, preparing to answer some very key questions will help in the process:

1. What kind of leader do I want to be?

2. Will I choose to make service a key part of my leadership, and if so, how? How will I choose to perform in service to others?

3. How will I strike the proper balance between the exercise of moral and positional authority?

4. How will I go about the task of creating, building, and nurturing others as a team?

5. When I am pressed for time to respond to a difficult situation, what core values and beliefs about leadership will I call upon to help me/those I lead to get through the challenge?

6. How will I make others around me, and the business that I serve, better because of my leadership?

7. By what measures will I hold myself accountable for the success, or lack of success, of the team?

8. How will I help the people that I lead become successful and fulfilled in their career aspirations?

9. What is my ultimate goal as a leader? What purpose do I want to fulfill, and what contribution do I want to make?

As you reflect on your answers to these questions, you essentially have begun to build a vision for your leadership journey. This creates a picture of the world you want to build, the mountain you need to prepare to climb and the impact that you envision having in your world. In other words, you have created the 'why' and the reasons behind this journey.

Now, in all seriousness, if you found yourself skimming over these questions and not putting much thought into them, we would encourage you to stop. You should reread the questions and give yourself the opportunity to reflect here. Then, you should write the answers down because they become a key component to your leadership map later on.

Figuring out what fuels your passions and what crushes your soul will act as your compass, leading you along your path throughout this quest. Figure out what you're good at and what you're not so good at. Keep it simple. Do more of what you're good at and less of everything else.

"A journey of a thousand miles, begins with a single step." – Lao Tzu

Coaching Corner (Coach Tim)

It's critically important as a leader that you create an environment where it's safe for others to be truthful. As a leader, you will want to hear the truth for several reasons:

- To get an accurate view of your brand, performance, and reputation.
- To deeply understand how others perceive you.
- To identify your blind spots so you can own them.
- To get clarity on issues early, so you can address them before it's too late, too hard, or too expensive to resolve.
- To demonstrate to those sharing information that you will not take it personally.
- To assess whether your communication skills create lift or frustration in others.

CHAPTER 2:
Habits of a
Fired-Up Leader

"Don't be afraid to give up the good and go for the great."
— *Steve Prefontaine*

At our organization we have a tagline we often use: **Get Up –
Show Up – Fire Up – Own It!** It shows up on our team's email
signatures and many of our T-shirt designs. Like other solid
taglines, this statement has significance to us and what it means for
those of us working diligently on our leadership:

- **"Get Up"** is the moment you decide to be intentional as you
  undertake the path ahead.
- **"Show Up"** speaks to the defining traits that will cause you to
  stand out from the crowd.
- **"Fire Up"** is all about how you will impact the world around you
  through your leadership.
- **"Own It"** is about taking responsibility for your attitudes,
  actions and behaviors while you get the job in front of you
  accomplished.

Leading yourself well, the simple act of 'showing up', is made up
of traits that will make a difference. These foundational traits will be
ever present. These are at the heart of a leader becoming successful,
long lasting, and impactful. These simple habits, in theory, are not
easy to obtain and maintain, but will cause you to stick out from the
crowd.

> *"There is only one corner of the universe you can be certain
> of improving, and that's your own self." – Aldous Huxley*

The Habits of the Fired-Up Leader:

- Be Values Driven
- Own Your Attitude
- Be Willing to Stretch
- Be Hungry
- Lean into the Pressure
- Take Responsibility
- Fail Well and Finish Strong

We will explore these habits in depth throughout this book. But to get started, let's explore them individually at a high level.

#1 - Be Values Driven

We all live by values. However, the reality for many of us is that we haven't spent enough time identifying what these values are or how to make choices that are connected to them. As a result, we find ourselves on "cruise control' as we work through our life. Unfortunately, this style of operating simply will not work when it comes to leadership.

You must spend time reflecting on the most critical and important values to you. This process, on the one hand, can be a daunting task, often forcing you to be intentional and come to points of decision and clarity. On the other hand, it also becomes a process that once done, creates a tremendous resource to assist you in your ability to navigate your leadership quest and all the challenges and opportunities that will be presented to you.

Here is the challenge: we all come to our values from different paths. There is nothing truly in common between each of our sets of values. We gain them from times of reflection, challenge or experience. Sometimes it seems we inherit them (and accept them) from our families or people we consider as role models.

Regardless of the path you've taken to identify the values that will guide you, it becomes critical to your leadership quest that you choose your own values, make them your own, and adapt them to your unique being. You have your own goals, strengths and views. In order to fully leverage values for your leadership journey, they must fit you or you risk acting and behaving with inconsistencies to your core.

Your quest and the journey ahead will be filled with thousands, if not millions, of choices. The way you make them will reflect the values you have, and it won't be long before the people around you quickly see how you operate and what is important to you. If you state you value one thing, but operate differently, it will destroy the trust people have in you and your leadership status.

Choosing what matters is hard. This is particularly true when you find yourself in leadership and experience the many voices of others attempting to influence your path. Choosing what matters has consequences. Most of us struggle to choose what matters most to us because we don't have a framework on which to base our decision. That framework needs to be built on your defined and committed value set.

In life, we often default to the obvious or safe choice. Your values framework will allow you to consistently and consciously choose what matters most. The process helps you get to the heart and soul of the matter, choosing the best path forward.

Bottom line here: take the time to really define your values, build your leadership brand around these values and hold yourself accountable that every decision you make will be grounded in them.

🔥 Coaching Corner (Coach Chris & Coach Tim)

From our experience with clients, the development of values and putting these values into meaningful statements that can be used in daily practice can be extremely challenging. The process, although personal and individual in nature, can often be more productive and facilitated by using a coach to assist you with exploring, focusing and finalizing your values statements.

Your coach will also naturally become a valuable resource in assisting you to stay accountable to the values you land on. We encourage you to get a coach if you don't have one already.

Reach out the "Fired-Up Team" to explore your coaching options! www.firedupculture.com/executive-coaching

> *"Do your work with your whole heart, and you will succeed - there's so little competition." – Elbert Hubbard*

#2 - Own Your Attitude

 Your enthusiasm and energy will differentiate you from the crowd. Enthusiasm (like steam in a boiler) when controlled and turned on, starts the wheels of machinery into action.
Do you "bring it" in every opportunity? Let's reflect for a moment. Here are two scenarios for you to consider.

1. When you arrive at a meeting, are the people you're meeting with excited to see you?

2. When your name shows up on someone's phone as you call them, what's their reaction?

Both of these examples are measurements of the level of energy you're giving off and the impact it has on your relationships. Have you become a drain on the people around you, or do you light up the room when you enter? Enthusiasm becomes contagious. As a leader, you need to find ways to 'bring it'. Those around you will thank you for it, too.

(Coach Chris)

Let me give you a quick high-impact example of what I mean by a 'Bringing It' attitude. A few years back, I spent many days coaching youth sports, baseball and basketball in particular. This tends to happen when you're raising four children. Youth sports is a fantastic training ground for young adults and also a great place to practice leadership.

One of the most memorable teams I had the privilege of coaching was named "The Heat". As you can see, the 'fired-up' theme has been around for a while. This team of boys aged 12 to 14 have now grown into adults. They're getting married, raising families and have remained true and long-lasting friend of my oldest son, Gabe.

"The only disability in life is a bad attitude." – Scott Hamilton

There are a couple of things that have lingered from this chapter of their lives, beyond the friendships.

The first is one of my favorites. When I see these men today, they still call me "Coach". I appreciate that because it tells the story for me of how my leadership has impacted them. Their words are given out of affection and appreciation. Truly my definition of influence.

The second thing that always gets referenced by this group of men is a small saying we had as a team. "Let's Go Heat". And the chant went on: (H) Hunger, (E) Energy, (A) Attitude and (T) Teamwork. It was created at the time to focus us as a group, but it also was a call to action for us as individuals. Were you willing to bring the HEAT?

The funny part of the "Let's Go Heat" story is that these men chanted it loudly during the celebration speeches at Gabe's wedding. It was hilarious and satisfying to each of us who were part of that experience and it continues to bond us today.

Enthusiasm does not necessarily mean a person who is a cheerleader. It's a leader who exudes confidence in the path and a shared belief that the ultimate goal will be attained despite any challenges that may arise. It's about perseverance. It's about messages of positive affirmation.

You can provide significant lift to your team during all steps of the process just by tapping into your own enthusiasm. Enthusiasm provides inspiration and clarity and fuel for the team, especially when the ultimate goals may be difficult or foggy to see, at best.

The case can be made that enthusiasm and energy are synonymous. We see projects and activities that range from high interest and those that will fail to capture attention.

Your role in bringing positive energy to each part of the project ensures the eventual intended outcomes: engagement and results. The ability you demonstrate when framing a challenging or uninteresting piece of the work in a positive light can create profound energy.

(Coach Tim)

I was once at the start of a hiking trail in a park in Lane Country, Oregon. I was preparing for a short hike to a viewpoint known as "Spencer Butte". I witnessed a grandmother in the process of preparing six grandchildren, aged 7 to 14, for an outing to see the top.

Four of the young children were excited and enthusiastically joining in the preparations, which included making lunches and packing up clothes. One child seemed a bit scared by the impending adventure, and a 12-year-old boy was frowning and making surly responses under his breath about what they were doing and how stupid it was.

I was struck by how much this band of intrepid grandchildren mirrored the team in the company our consulting firm had just worked with. It all started off as enthusiasm, trepidation and negative aptitudes at the beginning, with the ultimate outcome of the experience yet to be determined.

Observing the grandmother at work, I first noticed her energy and the way she went about explaining all of the preparations and how those would make this adventure more enjoyable. Although she was clearly a seasoned leader of grandchildren, she was very aware of the fear and negative attitudes that were present on the fringes of the expedition. She observed that, if left unchecked, these could very well infect the others and diminish, if not ruin, a promising outing.

She was gentle in her approach to bring the two reluctant children into the fold. With reassurance, she helped the scared girl understand what was in store for her, and that she wouldn't want to miss out on this experience this with her siblings. An older brother was enlisted to help her and a smile soon appeared on her face. This left only the 12-year-old naysayer as an outlier of the group.

After encouragement and pointing out what might be fun about the outing, the young man protested that he wanted to stay in the car and play video games. What happened next was an example of leadership worthy of admiration and imitation.

Having concluded the preparations, she brought the kids together in a circle, and with a smile and a firm voice full of conviction she addressed the "team" with the following words.

"Today we are climbing a mountain! At the top is the most beautiful view of the countryside and fun rocks you can climb and explore. This adventure is only going to be its best if we're all in it together, taking care of one another and helping each other where we can. When we come down after eating your lunch and playing at the top, you will have accomplished something, together."

She then put her arm around the young boy who had been so negative and, instead of punishing or scolding him, said quietly, while looking him in the eye, "We all are going on this adventure and you're going to love it! I need you to help your siblings and be a leader today, can you do that for me?"

In mere moments, without using her positional authority at all, she had reframed the experience for the team. She had reassured the person that was scared, empowered everyone on the team to help and support the others, and refocused the naysayer into a positive influence on the task ahead with a set of clearly defined responsibilities. And all of that before lunch!

I chose to follow them, hearing the positive and excited voices talking about the trail, the animals, an eventually, the view. When the summit had been achieved, she offered praise to the group and individually to each child and the role they had played.

As they returned to their van, you could see that by creating an atmosphere of positive anticipation and a supportive culture, the great experience and accomplishment was shared by all. There is a great deal to be learned from such leaders... from such grandmothers.

Let's be clear. A team is in a very dangerous place when its leader loses their energy for the work. It's critically important for you to consistently check your own energy and enthusiasm for the work at hand. Are you leaning in or out? Be intentional about how you're projecting your enthusiasm to those around you. It can really make a big difference. When you consider your role as an influencer, bringing energy and a positive feeling to the team is essential.

 Coaching Corner (Coach Tim)

Keep these thoughts in mind as you climb the steps of leadership. The quest to becoming the leader you're called to be has many steps and turns.

- The higher you go, the longer it takes.
- The higher you go, the higher the level of commitment.
- The higher you go, the easier it is to lead.
- The higher you go, the greater the growth.

#3 - Be Willing to Stretch

The quest you're on, simply put, will have moments of frustration and challenge that come along with the times of joy and celebration. At the core of the journey is a willingness to stretch beyond your comfort zone. You need to stretch beyond what you already know, look at your world differently and be willing to often step into the unknown.

In order to become a leader of influence, we must first possess a willingness to invest in leadership growth, regardless of the circumstances that might be unfolding around us. The willingness to learn at every opportunity and to embrace each challenge is the secret of success. When faced with the choice to grow, or to remain where you are, the answer should be clear: grow!

The mindset of willingness, which allows you to embrace challenges and look for the opportunities within, is a cornerstone of dynamic and impactful leadership.

"Do the one thing you think you cannot do. Fail at it. Try again. Do better the second time. The only people who never tumble are those who never mount the high wire. This is your moment. Own it." – Oprah Winfrey

#4 - Be Hungry

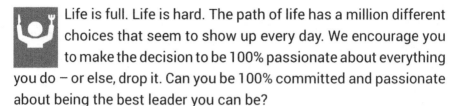 Life is full. Life is hard. The path of life has a million different choices that seem to show up every day. We encourage you to make the decision to be 100% passionate about everything you do – or else, drop it. Can you be 100% committed and passionate about being the best leader you can be?

Great leaders are grown, not born. Just like a highly successful artist or athlete, watch the performance of leadership around you. This will help you to gain insight into how to improve your own skills. Making yourself a student of leadership will serve you well.

Just like a person who is learning a musical instrument, leadership actions, self-reflection and the study of leadership, require practice. Students who engage in regular practice with their chosen instrument improve at a much more rapid pace than those who only play sporadically. The same is true for growing leaders.

Find opportunities to purposefully place yourself in situations. Read case studies, get into conversations and mentoring relationships with other successful leaders, and choose to make the effort to improve. Being hungry and finding ways to feed that hunger will begin to reap rapid rewards for your efforts. Your growth will also become very apparent to others.

> *"The tragedy of life is often not in our failure, but rather in our complacency; not in our doing too much, but rather in our doing too little; not in our living above our ability, but rather in our living below our capacities." – Benjamin E. Mays*

#5 - Lean In

"Lean into the pressure" is a phrase that reminds us that, while our most natural and initial instinct is to pull away and avoid situations that will make us uncomfortable, leadership of self requires the opposite. Just as first responders move toward danger as others flee, as an effective leader you have to become the person who embraces difficulties and challenges as a matter of daily course. This is not an innate behavior in most people. The natural tendency to avoid discomfort must be overcome.

As a leader, train yourself to move toward things that are distressing and uncomfortable.

Knowing that problems or challenging situations rarely, if ever, satisfactorily resolve themselves, provides the underlying rationale for why leaders must "lean into the pressure".

Whether it's conflict among team members, the changing of a long-held system that is not working, or a lack of capacity on the part of the team to perform their work, things will only get better if we decide to lean in. This famous saying sums it up well:

"Avoidance means... that we will pay twice."

It's always best to address an issue in a timely manner. Don't just hope that it will magically improve on its own.

Changing the mindset of perceiving "challenges as obstacles" and replacing it with the perception of "challenges as opportunities" is foundational to the successful leader. This acquired skill set will serve the future leader at every step moving forward. It will also eventually become a distinguishing characteristic of your leader brand. With a commitment to "leaning in", you will experience opportunities at every turn.

"Even the darkest night will end, and the sun will raise." – Victor Hugo

#6 - Take Responsibility

 Let me be direct: we're living in times of unprecedented complexity. As a result, it can be challenging to get the best out of people. There seem to be two paths that leaders follow:

1. Leaders who deflect blame and are masters of "learned helplessness".
2. Leaders who take responsibility for their own behaviors, decisions, and attitudes.

You need to be the responsible leader and choose the second path. Be the one who is willing to identify the challenges and be part of the solution. Instead of spreading blame, take ownership for your part and address the issues...head on. Take responsibility.

While all our actions as leaders in some way determine whether we will earn trust, how we do or do not take responsibility for our behaviors and actions has the greatest influence on our ability to build, earn, and grow trust.

Put very simply: if you haven't earned trust from your stakeholders, you won't be able to get things done and advance your organization to greater impact. Choose to take responsibility as the leader. Own the problem, take a hard-nosed approach, present a solution, get to work, and don't make the same mistake twice. You'll stave off disaster, fix problems faster, build trust, and achieve better results.

> *"Owning our story and loving ourselves through that process is the bravest thing that we'll ever do." – Brené Brown*

Coaching Corner (Coach Chris)

I want to encourage you to behave like an adult. I know that may seem straightforward but think about it. In our workplaces, when there is challenge and angst, it usually happens because someone is behaving poorly. The very core of being an adult is all about taking responsibility. Here are some steps towards taking greater responsibility:

Be responsible for who you are.
Be responsible for what you can do.
Be responsible for what you have received.
Be responsible for those you lead.

#7 - Fail Well and Finish Strong

A person's life is just a collection of experiments. We're meant to enjoy them and grow from them. If you learn to love the process of experimentation, the prospect of failure isn't so scary anymore.

While moving through your leadership journey, it's extremely easy to find yourself fatigued, frustrated and settling for less. A quest will do that to you. When you hit those moments and you're ready to throw up your hands in defeat, keep at the forefront of your thoughts the importance of "failing well" and "finishing strong".

In theory, these could be two separate habits. But we look at them as very much connected and we've intentionally listed them together. Although it seems intuitive, the learned discipline to follow through and bring every aspect of a task or project to conclusion, is critical.

In business, the mantra of *"90% done is not done at all"*, applies most of the time. Establish your own personal compass and systems that will allow you to stay on track and finish the quest. You will quickly get noticed.

The next most important habit of your personality is your flexibility, i.e., your mental attitude, or lack thereof. If you demonstrate flexibility, you have the ability to adjust to any and all circumstances (even when failure shows up) without losing your composure.

Regular self-reflection is a final and necessary step to finishing well. In fact, we recommend making this habit a final step in any project. The commitment to "debrief" and analyze every aspect of a project is critical for learning and leads to improvement.

Great leaders create a structure that allows for regular critical examination of performance, searching for areas of improvement and opportunities for change.

If you're going to fail, remember to fail well by learning from your mistakes, then keep heading toward the finish line.

> *"What you do today can improve all your tomorrows." – Ralph Marston*

🔥 Coaching Corner (Coach Tim)

When it comes to building success from failure, no one did it better than Thomas Edison, the famous inventor who is most notably credited with inventing the lightbulb.

Edison took a lesson from every misstep in his life. He was not going to let circumstances decide his fate. Today, we all know him as a great inventor, but it took him nearly 1,200 tries to perfect the lightbulb.

If you asked him about his lightbulb invention though, he would say, "I haven't failed, I've just found over 1,000 ways that do not work." Throughout his 84 years, Edison acquired 1,093 patents. Now, that really is the definition of failing and finishing well!

CHAPTER 3: Chart Your Course - The Brand is You

"No matter how far you have gone on a wrong road, turn around." – *Turkish Proverb*

As you continue along your leadership journey quest, you need to make the commitment to assess your strengths and areas for growth that will become the cornerstone for your future success. Now is the time. We find many clients just talk about *doing* the right things. But the most successful clients actually *do* the right things. As Nike would say, "Just Do It".

Leadership at its core is about service. This requires leaders to be intently self-aware with regard to their own level of relational ability, professional expertise, organizational skill, communicative capacity, and emotional intelligence. These are foundational skills that must be recognized and nurtured in order to effectively "lead yourself" and others.

But a word of caution: it's not just a case of grabbing the next self-help book or listening to the latest podcast. We need to understand, with clarity, how we're 'showing up' in our behaviors, attitudes and actions – the good, the bad and the ugly – so we can decide what we're going to do about it.

It's critical for your leadership growth to increase your awareness of our impact on others. This feedback provides specifics areas and themes for potential coaching and development activities as you move forward.

If you're a leader that aspires to be effective in all of the aforementioned areas, the willingness to be self-critical means committing to a lifestyle of growth, reflection and humility. These qualities will manifest themselves in the actions of self-improvement, life-long learning, and service to others.

When the question of "Would you work for you?" is considered at the most basic level, leading yourself in the most effective manner possible is the logical first step. As you move toward roles, opportunities and responsibility of greater influence over others, your individual "house" must be in great order.

We've all had the experience of working for a leader that we greatly admire. Such leaders appear to lead with ease. They appear to be on the pulse of each area of the organization. The day-to-day tasks and the long-term vision for the company seem to blend seamlessly.

Such leaders know the names of the team members and seem to be able to connect with and support them instinctively. In short, they are able to make everyone around them feel better and perform more efficiently. Their actions instill confidence in the team and all the team members to contribute in ways they may not have thought possible.

Then there is the other experience as well. Most all of us have also had to endure a time when the person in charge was lacking. They seemed to drain energy from the organization for their own personal needs or goals. To these individuals, positional authority was more important than support and competence applied to the job at hand.

As a result of how these individuals were 'showing up', productivity waned, morale suffered, and results were flat. It's in these moments you begin to experience team members "voting with their feet", electing to leave or change teams. Those who remain will settle into a place of working, endure and surviving the "working environment".

Thriving and empowerment are nowhere to be found. What could be a culture of deeply meaningful interactions and purpose becomes a collection of transactions and compliance exercises.

In contrast, when effective leaders are studied, a set of themes very quickly emerges. These leaders have developed habits, personal commitments and self-discipline that directly underpin their ability to be effective in the leadership role. They distill this concept to its very essence; they are highly effective at leading themselves.

These leaders describe themselves as the most organized person that they know and have developed systems to enhance their effectiveness. These leaders are nearly unanimous in their assertion that positive relationships and nurturing those relationships comes first.

They commit to the support and nurturing of their team and the next generation of leaders. It's exceptionally rare that such leaders "make things up as they go along", or "shoot from the hip". These leaders make commitments that drive their behavior, and they lead themselves as effectively as they are perceived to lead others.

> *"Love your whole story even if it hasn't been the perfect fairy tale." – Melanie Moushigian Koulouris*

Coaching Corner (Coach Chris & Coach Tim)

We encourage you to pause for a moment and really take a meaningful look at how intentional you've been at assessing yourself and the way you're 'showing up' impacts those around you.

At *Fired Up Culture*, we are firm believers in the power of assessments. We use several in our coaching practice, including the Birkman Assessment, StrengthsFinder and our firms Leadership360, Own It and Emergent Leaders assessment processes.

As you undergo your quest for leadership, an assessment can provide valuable insights into your strengths, passions and needs that will propel you toward success. By creating a greater depth of understanding of your uniqueness, increasing your language to talk about who you are and what you're all about and to be intentional in the decisions you make, you will find yourself increasing the speed of your leadership journey.

Visit www.wouldyouworkforyou.com/resources for more information.

Discover Your Style and Voice

Leadership styles are often discussed as though they were fashions or trends. Specific styles of leadership are actually the different opportunities for applications of the fundamentals of leading others, teams and culture.

Below are descriptors of some of the most recognizable ways in which leadership is described. Somewhere, or through some combination, you may find your most dominate leadership style. While people may perceive that a leader uses one style or application more frequently than others, the careful observer will notice that skillful and successful leaders use all of the listed styles/applications to bring about consistent and meaningful results.

Like a language, your leadership voice is an active display of your values, principles, beliefs and the way you connect and communicate with those around you.

Effective leadership, applied with intentionality and eagerness, is sometimes described as "situational leadership". Frequently used, yet not fully understood by most people, situational leadership is the learned ability of a leader to recognize and analyze the needs at hand. You need to recognize the leadership application that will be most effective for any given situation.

The challenge here for most of us is that we have our own strengths and ways of doing things, but these might not be highly effective or well received by those around us. So, how do we find the right balance and maintain integrity and confidence in our unique leadership voice?

"Situational leadership" is not formulaic. The "situation" simply presents you with a set of variables from which the best "blend" of leadership strategies can be applied. The careful and thoughtful application of leadership can remove barriers and areas of resistance from the tasks and processes at hand. The proper choice and application of the situational leadership options will build up our relational "bank accounts", create positive reserves and ensure more efficient and effect results. In short, if you lead thoughtfully, the team will be more engaged, connected and will work harder.

In our work with a very diversified group of global organizations, we've found that most are very open and encouraging of varied approaches to leadership, provided they do not violate established values and norms. Some entities, however, have a favored model of leadership that is used repeatedly, whether or not it brings about the results that are desired.

The famous psychologist, Abraham Maslow, once said, *"If the only tool you have is a hammer, you will start treating all of your problems like a nail."* This is an apt descriptor for a single leadership style employed repeatedly and without reflection.

Training yourself to be a student of leadership allows you the opportunity to move between leadership styles in the most effective manner possible. It will also create the ability to fully leverage your individual strengths and make choices that best fit the environments you want to lead in.

Coaching Corner (Coach Chris)

I am passionate about golf. It's one of my personal sanctuaries and is how I take care of myself. Even as a lifelong golfer, I continue to learn my own tendencies.

My 'game' looks really different from everyone else. But despite the differences we all bring to the game, there are some things that remain true for all of us. We each have clubs in our bag and it's up to us to select the right one at the right time.

A golfer uses different clubs for different distances and trajectories of shots.

In the same way, as a skillful leader, you not only need to be aware of different leadership styles, but we also want to encourage you to train yourself in the use, pacing and proper selection of the necessary leadership style for the right circumstances.

> *"There is no passion to be found playing small -*
> *in settling for a life that is less than the one you*
> *are capable of living." – Nelson Mandela*

Levels of the Fired-Up Leader

As you continue along your leadership quest, we want to acknowledge that there are several levels of leadership, and depending on your experiences to date, you could find yourself sitting currently within any of them.

It's the objective of the quest to continue your journey and find the opportunities to move up the levels. Sometimes our clients find this happening quickly, while others can take a long time. You also may find yourself sitting at a particular level for an extended period of time as you develop your skills and take on more responsibility.

We have included some specific action items to focus on for each of the five leadership levels (stated below). By engaging these, you will find sustained success as you move from one level to the next. Make sure you continue these activities, even when you've moved onto the next level of leadership.

Level #0: The Practitioner

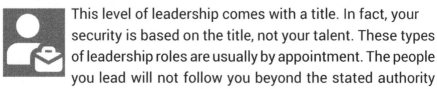 We've included this as a 'pre-level' to the leadership journey. For most professionals, we develop our skills in the areas of being a strong practitioner or technician. Some people find themselves staying in the practitioner level and never moving towards other leadership roles.

Coaching Corner

- Get to know yourself well; your strengths, needs and stress responses.
- Focus on the development and consistent execution of your craft.
- Look for and take on projects that force you out of your comfort zone.
- Begin evaluating your desire for taking on potential leadership opportunities.

Level #1: The Position

This level of leadership comes with a title. In fact, your security is based on the title, not your talent. These types of leadership roles are usually by appointment. The people you lead will not follow you beyond the stated authority that comes with your title. You'll find yourself being more challenged with volunteers, white-collar works and the younger workforce.

Coaching Corner

- Know your job.
- Connect people to the history of the organization.
- Accept responsibility.
- Do your job with excellence.
- Offer creative ideas for change and improvement.

Level #2: The Connector

 This level of leadership is getting people to work for you when they are not obligated to do so. This type of leadership begins with the heart, not the head. It's all about building amazing one-on-one relationships.

It leads to stronger interpersonal relationships. There is no pecking order to decide who is number one, but in fact, it's all about talent development. Your time, energy, and focus are placed on your team members' needs and desires.

People who can't develop, sustain and build solid relationships will be unable to sustain leadership roles at this level.

Coaching Corner

- Develop and live by a strong set of foundational values and leadership principles.
- Possess a genuine love for people.
- Make those around you more successful.
- See things through other people's eyes.
- Include others in the journey.
- Love people more than procedures.
- Do 'win-win' or don't do it at all.
- Deal wisely with difficult people.
- Own and consistently live out the principles of the 'Emergent Leader' (more on this to come).

> *"When we are foolish, we want to conquer the world. When we are wise, we want to conquer ourselves." – John C. Maxwell*

Level #3: The Coach

 This level of leadership is the "results level". People coming together as a team to accomplish a purpose. It's about being a true team; coaching and building a collaborative team of people while maximizing the strengths of individuals. A team that is united and focused to drive meaningful business impact and results.

Coaching Corner

- Initiate and accept responsibility for results.
- Develop and follow a statement of purpose.
- Develop accountability for results, beginning with you.
- Know and do the things that give you high returns.
- Communicate the strategy and vision of the organization.
- Become a 'change agent'.
- Make the difficult decisions that will make a difference.

Level #4: The Culture Champion

 This level of leadership is where true leadership is recognized for several factors. The focus is on consistent superior performance and the creation of the next generation of leaders. The entire organization is positively impacted by level 4 leadership.

Coaching Corner

- Recognize that people are your most valuable asset.
- Place priority of developing people.
- Be a model for others to follow.
- Pour your leadership efforts into the top 20% of people.
- Expose key leaders to growth opportunities.
- Be able to attract other winners and producers to the common goal.
- Surround yourself with an inner core of people who compliment your leadership.

To assist you in moving from one level to the next, our work in the **Would You Work for You Series** is specifically designed around several of these steps along your leadership quest. Here are some examples:

- Permission Leadership is the primary focus of the next book in this series, **The Connector**. Through the pages of The Connector, we explore the process of leading others, one relationship at a time.
- In the third resource in the series, **The Coach**, we dive deep into teaming and leveraging a team coaching model to impact and drive business results. *The Coach* is focused on Level 3 Leadership: Teaming for Results.
- And finally, when you achieve Level 4 Leadership, People Development, we have the ability to build and ignite a fully engaging workplace culture. At level 4, your leadership becomes the **Culture Champion**.

By the way, it goes without saying that in order to move into the next level of leadership, you must have already mastered the skills of the previous level. Mastery is where the necessary thoughts, actions and influence are second nature. Part of your leadership quest is to master each of the levels and progressively move onto the next.

"Every great dream begins with a dreamer. Always remember, you have within you the strength, the patience, and the passion to reach for the stars to change the world." – Harriet Tubman

Becoming an Emergent Leader

When it comes to being an effective Level 2 Leader, **the Connector**, this is about becoming the Emergent Leader. 'Emerging' is an interesting and intentional word. By definition, it means "to move out of, or away from and come into view. To become visible." The Emergent Leader, as we like to call it, is an intentional act or set of acts to lead.

Self-identifying leaders, leaders who have the courage to step forward with the "skills, instincts and personality traits" at precisely the right time are what we call: *Emergent Leaders.* To be an Emergent Leader, you don't have to have a title of 'Manager' or 'Supervisor'. Emergent Leaders can be anyone who has the knowledge and skills to add value, enhance a system or fill a gap. In short, Emergent Leaders step forward where leadership is needed.

EMERGENT LEADERS

Emergent Leaders do five key things which enable them to take leadership at the appropriate time. They: (1) Coach, (2) Offer Counsel, (3) Connect People to Resources, (4) Encourage Stewardship, and (5) Help Others See the Big Picture.

Emergent Leaders *Coach*

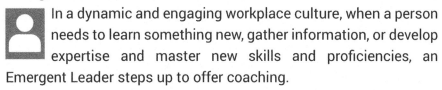

In a dynamic and engaging workplace culture, when a person needs to learn something new, gather information, or develop expertise and master new skills and proficiencies, an Emergent Leader steps up to offer coaching.

Emergent Leaders *Offer Counsel*

Once people turn their attention toward solving job-related problems and making day-to-day workplace decisions, Emergent Leaders make themselves available to offer counsel. This therefore means people can find their own solutions to everyday issues and problems.

Emergent Leaders *Connect People to Resources*

Having learned how to make decisions and solve problems independently, people in a Responsibility Culture begin to seek the resources they need to complete projects independently. Emergent Leaders connect their coworkers to the resources they need to meet these challenges.

Emergent Leaders *Encourage Stewardship*

Having mastered the art of securing resources, people are ready to assume ownership for their jobs and for the systems they work in. Emergent Leaders encourage their coworkers to become stewards of the organization.

Emergent Leaders *Help Others See the Big Picture*

Every member of a Responsibility Culture needs to understand how his or her job supports the larger purpose of the organization. To help make this important link, Emergent Leaders help their colleagues see the big picture by understanding how their individual and combined efforts contribute to the organization's success.

Coaching Corner (Coach Chris)

We dive much deeper into the practice of being an Emergent Leader in the second book of the *Would You Work for You* series, *the Connector*. However, it's also important to mention here that every attitude, behavior and practice we recommend you put into place for leading yourself well is designed to also set you on a course to transition to leading others well. The bridge between leading yourself and leading others is the Emergent Leader.

Leading yourself well, with depth, consistency and intentionality, is a must.

And then a shift happens. You become a connector. A connector of people. It's that space where you move from being focused on yourself to a focus on the needs of those around you.

What's it going to take for you to become an Emergent Leader?

"Lack of direction, not lack of time, is the problem." – Zig Ziglar

Moving from Practitioner to Influencer

One of the most challenging times for a person's career is a move from being a successful practitioner to leading. In whatever profession, technical area, or trade, we all begin as a practitioner. It's how you learn the role. Apart from those who arrive in a position of authority through inheritance or family connection, you first "learn the ropes" in terms of progressing from novice to highly skilled technician, then you master your craft. This is the path which the great majority of people take. Many people then stay in this line of work for their entire careers.

Here's the problem though: the skills needed to be successful as a practitioner are substantially different than those required for effective leadership. The transition space between these two worlds is one that many struggles with and often fail at completing. Simply said, expertise alone in a particular field does not qualify nor prepare you for leadership.

"Do you want to know who you are? Don't ask. Act! Action will delineate and define you." – Thomas Jefferson

Coaching Corner (Coach Tim)

I want to do a quick introduction to my client, Ariana. During our coaching process, one of the areas Ariana was working through was the struggle moving from being a very successful individual contributor, to a leader of others.

Ariana found herself thrown into the leadership transition essentially overnight. She wondered if she'd ever be successful as a manager and felt a bit of relief remembering how much easier her job was before she got the promotion. She felt a wash of worry nearly drown her as she took her seat at the table, feeling like a kid who finally gets to eat at the adult table on Thanksgiving.

As we walked through the situations she was dealing with, I shared a few thoughts with her.

"You're trying to be a piece of the team instead of leading your team to their goals. You have to let go of the tasks that aren't part of leadership. You've been picking up the slack, covering shifts, and taking over tasks when your team isn't performing. You need to take a step back and see that jumping in to do other people's jobs is only hurting *their* progress, and your *own* progress."

Ariana was being crushed under the weight of her new responsibilities, because she hadn't yet learned to let go of her previous duties. It was at this moment that Ariana decided to move toward becoming an Emergent Leader and owning the path ahead of her.

Understanding Positional vs. Moral Authority

There is a stark difference between the response of team members when following the "positional authority" of a manager (title), as opposed to the "moral authority" (values, principle, behaviors) of a leader. Your leadership quest needs to be more focused on influence rather than position.

Most of us do like titles and we usually receive these during a promotion or during the hiring process. Receiving a title, and the perception of positional authority that comes with it, is intoxicating. However, it often becomes a mask that prevents us from really owning and applying the necessary leadership practices.

We need to appreciate and understand that the "position" of leadership is just that. It's only a position until the moral authority of leadership is created. Committing yourself to developing the skills and capacity to lead effectively, combined with gaining the trust of those being led, is actually what defines your future effectiveness as a leader.

One additional point: it's quite common that positions of authority are assigned without the participation or input of those who will be led. Such decisions are rarely made with the support, praise or approval of actual team members. Most often a leader is simply chosen and placed into the role by superiors who are several steps removed from the team itself. Once again, this places the newly appointed leader in a position where attitudes, behaviors and actions that build relationships through influence become even more vital. Beginning with confidence is important, as is humility. Taking time to listen and connect with those you lead is particularly import when you're "placed" in the role.

> *"Don't wait for other people to be loving, giving, compassionate, grateful, forgiving, generous, or friendly... lead the way!"* – Steve Maraboli

Are You Creating Engagement or Compliance?

When you're being placed in a position of authority, you will also frequently be given a mandate/instruction. An example would be, "Get the team moving in the right direction."

It's important to remember that such mandates can create an exaggerated sense of urgency toward immediate actions. This is when you need to locate your 'pause button'.

Remember that no matter how urgent the need to "get moving" is, nothing replaces the fundamentals of first establishing positive relationships with team members. We also need to take a deeper look at the systems and support structures that are (or are not) in place prior to any attempts to create forward motion. In the long term, skipping the fundamentals will nearly always prove to be counterproductive.

As a leader, your goal is not merely the compliance of the team and their quiet acceptance of the direction. It's about earning and building engagement through loyalty and trust. Through an ongoing investment of time, demonstration of follow-through, and a commitment to helping remove barriers, productivity will improve and capacity will be built for the future.

Your ability to "move the team in the right direction" will be far more successful and sustainable if the incentive for such movement comes from the engagement of the people you're trying to lead. Remembering that "shared ownership" by the team, rather than "compliance" of the team, is the place where transformation can occur.

> *"The quality of a leader is reflected in the standards they set for themselves." –Ray Kroc*

Becoming the Complete Leader

Leading yourself well require a desire to learn, be vulnerable and show a willingness to open your mind to new ways of thinking. It also requires the individual to begin to acquire the knowledge and awareness of the organization's expectations and definitions of success for you as a leader.

As you move through the different levels of leadership, keep in mind that there are some common and connected behaviors that will help you be successful:

1. The willingness to learn with humility and genuine interest.

2. Being open to new ideas and showing the ability to process those though a set of highly developed core values.

3. Understanding that positive personal relationships are the bedrock of a leader's support and influence. Developing the ability to create and foster those relationships.

4. Training yourself to recognize, evaluate and adjust the organizational systems to support and empower those around you.

5. Showing a genuine interest in the success of others. Demonstrating empathy for their struggles and a willingness to support their growth.

6. The ability and willingness to listen, even in stressful situations.

7. Bringing individuals together as a team and helping them thrive. The ability to create a feeling of shared ownership in the project or outcome.

By being intentional about your learning and growth opportunities, or as we like to call it, "owning your career", your value as a team member rises and sets you apart from your peers.

A willingness to show initiative and go beyond is a clear a statement of your commitment. Show your energy, commitment and make yourself indispensable. This is the kind of leadership organizations really seek and teams thrive on.

> *"The key is to keep company only with people who uplift you, whose presence calls forth your best." – Epictetus*

Coaching Corner (Coach Tim)

Do you like to exercise? Well, I'm guessing about 1% of people reading this are probably going to say "Yes". But to the rest of us, as you work on your vulnerability, the process is very similar to beginning to work out at the gym.

It will be uncomfortable. It will leave you "sore" for a time period that is much longer than most people will appreciate.

As you move forward with resolve, you will be able to notice results in the form of small improvements. At the gym, these changes manifest in a change in appearance and fitness.

In the field of leadership, these show as noticeable changes in self-confidence, situational application of skills, and as a growing capacity for observation and analysis of the organization. It will become apparent to those around you that you have a growing capacity to take on more responsibility and are trusted to do so. You're demonstrating the ability to be present, real and trustworthy.

CHAPTER 4:
Get Naked - The Emotionally Present Leader

*"Authenticity requires
a certain measure of
vulnerability, transparency,
and integrity."*
– Janet Louise Stephenson

P ause.

Some of you may be confused by the title of this chapter. As long-time HR leaders, we want to be clear that we're not truly encouraging you to get naked at work! This will tend to be a short-term career choice that does not work well. However, it's our hope that the chapter title grabbed your attention, as this is an important topic.

Being transparent and vulnerable as a leader appears, on the surface, to be both simple and straightforward. The reality of being a leader who embodies these qualities requires a great deal of internal strength and a willingness to avoid momentary gains and affirmation for a longer-term structure for success.

Being "naked" (in other words, a willingness to be vulnerable and transparent) can create distinct advantages. One of the advantages is specifically in the areas of inclusion and collaboration. The collective ownership that comes from an open style of leadership allows for most challenges and opportunities to be collectively shouldered.

It allows for the feeling of success to be shared amongst the team, and it provides a place from where the leader can recognize and authentically celebrate the contributions of individual team members. This means honoring the individual, celebrating the individual and being 'real' at work.

A word of caution though. This path requires a strength of confidence, ego and personality. I know very few leaders who feel good when their ideas or authority appear to be openly challenged. When this happens, we're pulled to a place of slow reaction while positively facilitating conversations, all without taking personal offense. Putting forward an idea or a direction that draws criticism requires openness and courage. If real transparent collaboration is the intent, then the origin of a solution should be celebrated, regardless of where (or from whom) it came.

"Nakedness" and transparency of leadership can feel unsettling, even to the most experienced of leaders. Embracing the process of being real, i.e., being naked, is well worth the courage required and we encourage you to commit to the process.

> *"Be yourself — not your idea of what you think somebody else's idea of yourself should be." — Henry David Thoreau*

Showing Your Vulnerable Side

Vulnerability is still somewhat of an "off-limits" term in many workplaces. However, as more leaders and team members embrace their vulnerabilities, the workplace transforms into an environment of real connections, growth, increased trust, engagement, and respect. This list represents the future of the successful workplace.

All of us have vulnerabilities. It comes with being human. By concealing your vulnerabilities, you're essentially denying a major part of the real and authentic you from showing up. It also prevents you from connecting with others on a deeper level. This deeper level can lead to trustworthy relationships, increased collaboration, engagement and productivity.

We understand, and we want to you to understand as well, that being vulnerable means taking a risk. It can be daunting to do, but when we create a culture where all team members are willing to take the vulnerability plunge, everyone will benefit.

A core principle of self-leadership is the willingness to be vulnerable. To some, the word vulnerable may be strange, especially in a leadership context. This particular usage of the word implies a genuine openness to learning, critique and personal growth. It implies a willingness to examine your intent with your performance.

You may be thinking that vulnerability seems simple and straightforward. Just be real, be human. But along the journey, vulnerability will also be competing against showing value and that you're in control. Vulnerability takes an intentional effort to open up, share your thoughts and emotions while developing a "thick skin".

Embracing vulnerability can look different for all of us along this quest, but there are a few questions and steps to consider. Start by thinking about who you are at work and who you are at home and in other environments.

Are you the same person in both settings? As you wrestle with being more vulnerable, we encourage you to find consistency. Strive to be consistently the same authentic human in all that you do. Embrace your authentic true self, no matter the location or who you're meeting with and what the topic of discussion is.

The opportunity here is to directly connect our stories. The things we are passionate about, what we care for, what makes us excited, angry and challenged. Bring the real you and your story into the conversation. Team members want to work with a human, not a robot, and most people are excited to talk about their personal lives and emotions, either good or bad. Build connections with co-workers through real, honest conversations.

Having open, non-judgmental conversations fosters an environment of cohesiveness and teamwork where people feel they can share issues and ideas, both personal and professional, in a safe atmosphere. That emotion can also translate to the boardroom.

Don't be afraid to get invested and show emotion about a project or report. You might not always be successful but getting emotionally invested encourages others to do the same. This can then lead to a collective experience of excitement and connection.

We encourage you to be vulnerable. Take the risk. The rewards will be significant.

Coaching Corner (Coach Chris)

We want you to discover the correct level of leadership transparency and vulnerability. Here are for tips for leaning into being a more vulnerable leader:

- Own your story and be willing to share it.
- Get comfortable with your inexperience, lack of skills and shortcomings.
- Be curious and don't be defensive.
- Seek honest feedback.
- Hold things loosely and be willing to throw out your plans.
- Don't wait for perfect trust to exist.

"Shine with all you have. When someone tries to blow you out, just take their oxygen and burn brighter." – Katelyn S. Irons

A Plan for Growth

When taking on the challenges of leadership, you must do so with confidence. That being said, confidence tempered with humility and a genuine understanding of how much is still yet to be learned will serve any leader well. Personal change is learnable. Along your quest, it's equally important to develop the skills of 'unlearning' and identifying beliefs and behaviors that no longer serve us.

Leadership roles can be seen by some as a career accomplishment and an 'endgame' of sorts. In reality, it's a call to continue learning and growing, as well as serving. The dual tasks of delivering for others and continuing to grow professionally means seeking opportunities to broaden your knowledge, particularly in the aforementioned areas of positive working relationships, systems that serve, and building the capacity of others to perform. The truly wise leader knows that without continual growth, repetition of that we already know is all that can be accomplished.

> *"Setting goals is the first step in turning the invisible into the visible." – Tony Robbins*

Fuel for Growth:
Seeking Feedback and Being Coachable

You can't be your strongest without the brutal truth.
Being able to "hear" feedback implies far more than the ability to hear the words that are spoken. It describes a growth mindset of a leader that is receptive to suggestion and direction. Feedback that may be quite contrary to your current beliefs of self. As leaders, we need to be willing to seek and hear feedback from a wide range of sources opening ourselves up to potential criticism.

But just because we receive a message, it doesn't mean we have to accept it. We must take an active role in deciphering the information, making sense of it and taking responsibility for what we're going to choose to do with it. This is the tricky part. We need to approach this process by deploying our growth mindset versus being defensive.

Being able to sift through the feedback we receive and connect to the essence of the information is a skill that will allow an aspiring leader to grow. We need to be able to get to the themes we hear and then build our actions around those themes.

In our coaching practice, we provide 360-feedback for leaders. This is our tool and our process. It's eye opening, transformative and "painful". No one likes it, but everyone benefits from it. However, we can also tell you that even as a practitioner who is not emotionally tied to the information being conveyed, it's not uncommon for us to feel uncomfortable or challenged by trying to deliver the message.

One of the most effective strategies to assist with getting through this process and achieve true value and transformation is to focus on the themes and simplify the takeaways. Find the things you should be paying attention to and quickly get focused on what actions you could take.

Learn to exercise the muscles of giving and getting feedback. It will be a 'game changer' in your quest for leadership. But we also understand feedback can be extremely hard. This is because when you feel rejection and criticism and it hits you at the core, it shows you care about your work and you're pouring yourself into it. Frankly, if feedback stopped hurting, it would mean you had stopped caring.

Just as we commit to disciplines around our productivity and personal health systems that will better support a healthy lifestyle, reflection and analysis of feedback you receive should be no less intentional. In the world of academia, there is a saying that speaks to the need to hear, read, rewrite and re-read a piece of information eight or more times before it moves into long-term memory. It's only when something becomes committed to long-term memory that it then becomes usable.

For your leadership quest, this comes down to building your 'toolbox' of resources.

We encourage you to develop your own process for collecting, processing and using the information the world is giving to you. We encourage you to keep a journal. Now, I know for most of us, keeping a journal sounds like something you'd do back in junior high school.

But we're not taking about a locked journal you hide under your pillow. What we're encouraging is a process that encourages you to be curious, a listener, a seeker, reflective, and intentional.

Across history, many significant and impactful leaders have kept journals. These individuals came from all walks of life: inventors like Benjamin Franklin and Thomas Edison; world leaders like John Adams, Ronald Reagan, and Winston Churchill; and authors like Mark Twain and Ernest Hemingway.

Journaling and reflection, having a discussion with a trusted colleague or mentor, and taking time to think about the information intentionally, all provide you with a specific strategy. This can then be used to transform feedback and experiences into a powerful tool for growth and eventual transformation.

The journal or other learning systems and practices can become catalysts for positive movement in your life. A catalyst, as most of us know, is a chemical or compound which greatly speeds up or enhances a reaction between two or more chemicals, often releasing great energy in the process.

A person prepared with solid strategies and the mindset to see their world as a series of possibilities will quickly move beyond peers who are essentially stuck because they view daily toil as challenges and barriers versus the opportunities they provide.

Coaching Corner (Coach Tim)

The majority of us have had the experience of taking music lessons, participating in drama productions, or playing on a sports team. Unfortunately, in these environments, the people leading us are often "overly comfortable" providing very direct feedback with little regard for individual's feelings.

As a result of being dealt really direct feedback, many of us have become numb or non-responsive to the feedback. We learn to avoid situations or activities where feedback may be given. For many of us, this is why we dread the annual review process in our work.

It's mechanical and task driven. We don't position ourselves with the right mindset and the person delivering the feedback is often very uncomfortable delivering the news.

"There is no one giant step that does it. It's a lot of little steps." – Peter A. Cohen

---

Looking in the Mirror

Throughout our years of working with and studying leaders, one of the most important qualities that successful leaders possess is the ability to look realistically at their skill set. They make it a point to 'look in the mirror'.

We have just spent some time talking about feedback, and that is part of the process. But looking in the mirror goes beyond feedback. It truly is the act of self-reflection, assessment and a commitment to renewal. Across the board, they plan objectively with regard to how they will improve and do so in a way that is not self-deprecating. They have found ways of maintaining self-confidence, while working specifically on their desired areas of improvement. They do so with intentionality and attention. And they do so with a high degree of self-love and care.

You will need to inspire confidence from within. By the way, confidence isn't about convincing yourself through positive thinking that the failures, risks or dark shadows do not exist. Instead, confidence is knowing, beyond a shadow of a doubt, that regardless of how the risks you choose to take turn out, you will, in fact, be alright!

It can be exhausting, and at times, demoralizing, to make a concerted effort to constantly improve. Practicing and training relentlessly in areas that you're not naturally familiar with requires an inner commitment that most people don't have. Training this way means that discomfort and failure will be self-imposed conditions.

So, you may ask, what else do we derive from the practice of relentlessly training our weaknesses? One of the fruits of your labor is developing the ability to persevere and move forward, knowing that the ultimate goal is still in the future. It can often feel like a sports race.

For example, in the sport of professional cycling, there are some athletes that succeed just in one specific area of the discipline. They're exceptional sprinters, or they excel at the discipline of climbing thousands of feet upwards in the mountains. Some descend fearlessly and others demonstrate incredible endurance. The best of these has a level of strength in all of the phases of the sport. High-caliber cyclists have a saying of, "train your weaknesses and race your strengths."

Some of the most famous bicycle races are thousands of miles long and can last for weeks. The ability to endure and mentally overcome the short-term gratification for long-term objectives, even in the face of personal discomfort, sets leaders apart from the many who are waiting to be led.

Coaching Corner (Coach Chris)

I want you to pause and take a look in the mirror. Really take a good look at yourself. This exercise helps you to see your strengths and weaknesses. Make sure you stay kind to yourself while realistically assessing the areas you need to improve on.

- Have a conversation with yourself: what do you see? (Go ahead, no one is looking!)
- Name your strengths and weaknesses.
- Remember that you're the only one who can transform what you see in the mirror. When you see imperfections, find a way to build yourself up, not tear yourself down.

> *"We may encounter many defeats, but we must not be defeated." — Maya Angelou*

Being Coachable: Get Yourself a Board of Advisors

Every four years, images and footage from the Olympics stream into our homes. We sit in awe of the feats of strength, speed, and agility that we witness. An omnipresent feature of any competition is the television shot of the coach, who works with these amazingly talented athletes daily, watching their performance with great anticipation.

While omni-present in some activities, fields of endeavor, and the things we pursue, it's surprising how infrequently people who aspire to advance in their work career utilize a coaching resource. Wise people who wish to grow into a leadership position choose to access the services of a trusted individual to help guide them on their journey.

They are *willing* to be coached.

A trusted advisor can be a support that provides great returns, if as aspiring leaders we allow it to do so. When a coach is added to the team, and when combined with strong systems to support your goals, an aspiring leader can take on new challenges that might have seemed "out of reach" when going it alone.

As you read this section, we encourage you to ask yourself a question: do you tend to go at things alone or do you lean toward the comfort of seeking support?

Any married person would tell you that our spouses think that we lean toward doing it ourselves. You know those moments when you're lost and you have the choice to ask for directions, but you're not sure if you want to admit that you're actually lost? You get the picture.

Day after day, we see places where leaders would have greatly benefited from the wisdom, insight and learnings of others, rather than simply trying to do it by themselves. We're not suggesting that you need advisors for all aspects of your life. But it would be good to pause and be selective on the areas that could use good counsel.

Your "Board of Advisors" will significantly speed up your learnings while reducing the pain of trial, error and mistakes. Like a lifeline, a call to an advisor can move you through the needed thought process and your options for consideration much quicker than trying to accomplish the feat yourself.

A strategy that successful leaders often use when talking to a trusted advisor is "checking their perceptions". This process consists of sharing (with a trusted person) the thinking, processes and actions which have been used. When "checking the perception", the leader once again returns to a place of opening themselves up to feedback and critique from their advisor. Successful leaders engage in this process regularly, especially when decisions impact the direction of the organization or when the well-being of others is involved.

As an aspiring leader, we want to encourage you to begin employing this strategy of finding a coach and building a "Board of Advisors". It's a practice that forces you to engage in the discipline of hearing feedback, pressing on assumptions, critiquing decisions, examining communication and fostering a growth mindset. Utilizing a coach demonstrates the humility and awareness required to lead yourself, and others, effectively.

Coaching Corner (Coach Chris)

For years I have worked hard to become a better golfer. I love the game, even with its challenges and, frankly, frustrations. Just when you think you've got it figured out, you end up quickly realizing you don't.

As with most things in my life, I tend to lean toward being a self-learner and golf was no different. I read, I tried, I experimented, and, in some places, I improved dramatically. In others, however, I failed.

Being a self-directed learner is not a bad thing, and experience tells us you will eventually figure it out. The real question is: at what cost?

"Very often, a change of self is needed more than a change of scene." - A.C. Benson

CHAPTER 5:
Never-Ending Discipline

"Success is doing ordinary things extraordinarily well."
— Jim Rohn

L eading is a verb, so it should be filled with action. This action should be focused on and dedicated to the people you lead. When leaders realize this reality, they open the door for a different way of accomplishing business results through other people's results. Be the kind of leader for your team you'd be honored to follow and take steps to ensure you're giving the people you lead the time they need.

Highly successful leaders make the choice to be disciplined. We challenge you to find anyone that has been successful, and more importantly sustained it, who has not deployed never-ending discipline in how they move through the world. One aspect that is also present is the discipline to adhere to self-imposed commitments. You know – disciplines when there is no external pressure to do so.

The role of leadership impacts teams and people to such a great extent, that the discipline that a leader shows, particularly in their own personal habits, has a great deal to do with how impactful their work will be.

What appears to most as a relentless and perhaps unimaginable level of self-discipline, is really nothing more than a personal commitment to apply strategies of success, even to the most trivial of tasks. It takes a great deal less time to accomplish a waiting task proactively, rather than procrastinate and eventually deal with a situation that has worsened due to the delay.

As an example, think about your personal health. Would it not be easier to put disciplines in place that address issues early on, rather than waiting until you're sick, or the doctor gives you the dreaded diagnosis?

Leaders often find that it's far more efficient to deploy systems that help them stay focused, adjust their course and engage the things that are important to them. Expending unnecessary effort attempting to rectify an issue that could have been avoided, is simply nonsensical.

In short, a quality that we've observed most from successful leaders is the ability to employ highly efficient personal systems and organization strategies that keep them disciplined. They have found things that work, choose to live them and are consistently re-committing to them, no matter what's going on around them.

Coaching Corner (Coach Tim)

Small stuff, left unattended, becomes big stuff. For those in the process of growing personal leadership skills, "attention to detail" is the complete opposite of, "no worries... things will all work out on their own."

A word to the wise for you: there is nothing that actually takes care of itself or works out all on its own.

While some issues may appear to reach a level of resolution in the short term, unresolved communication or logistical challenges can be counted upon to reemerge and create future challenges for your leadership.

As leaders, it's important that we commitment to getting the "small stuff" done.

Attention to detail, quite simply, allows you as a leader to be more positive and nurturing of the people you serve. It goes without saying that there are very few effective leaders that employ a strategy of procrastination, dishonesty, or "wait and see".

> *"What you lack in talent can be made up with desire, hustle and giving 110% all the time." - Don Zimmer*

Be Purposeful in Your Steps

Let's not lose sight of the big picture. It's about results. Your ability to stay on a path that drives consistent results is the target. Results for yourself and results for the jobs you undertake. If you lose focus, you'll find yourself frustrated and fewer opportunities will come in your direction.

Individuals who consistently achieve their goals are purposeful in their steps. As you strive to be purposeful and results driven, we encourage you to be intentional around these six steps:

Step 1 - Define Success

Before you undertake any actions, be clear on the end result you're trying to achieve. Make defining success of everything you do intentional. If it's an organization defined objective, make sure you're clear on what success looks like from those who are in charge. Without a solid definition of success, you can find yourself reaching what you thought was the end result but end up in the wrong place.

Step 2 - Perform a Reality Check

Is the thing we're striving for realistic? What are the gaps between what you're experiencing today and what your preferred vision is? This reality check will assist your understanding of the steps that need to be taken.

Step 3 – Commit to the Mission

If your reality check shows you that you have a reasonable chance of getting where you want to go and you have access to the resources needed (time, talent, treasure, motivation, etc.) you have your defined mission. It becomes imperative that you commit to that mission.

Step 4 – Set the Goals

Set clear goals that can be measured and quantifiable. A few well-positioned milestones set the markers along your journey toward success. The goals set the smaller steppingstones required to get there. Any project or task you undertake for work or personal reasons should be broken down to this extent.

Step 5 – Define the Strategy

The strategy is all about effectiveness. The most effective way to get to your next goal. It defines the path you're going to take to get there. Like a good Google Map for your road trip, your strategy will guide you as you move forward.

Step 6 – Work the Plan

The plan simply boils down to what needs to be done. To what extend you need to define the plan will be influenced by the complexity of the strategy.

No matter your position or title, bringing assignments, tasks and objectives to completion is a mandatory skill, but this is particularly true for leadership. Bringing an idea from concept to reality requires you to be intentional in defining the necessary steps and owning those steps.

While this may seem overly simple, the ability of a leader to "own the details" is rarer than you might imagine. You're no longer just responsible for your results. Instead, you now have the responsibility to influence the success of an entire team of people.

As you work diligently to step into an ever-growing leadership presence, we encourage you to continue to deploy personal strategies for breaking large projects down into manageable objectives.

Don't forget one thing: if you can't consistently drive results, your leadership career will be short lived.

> *"Be willing to make decisions. That's the most important quality in a good leader. Don't fall victim to what I call the 'ready-aim-aim-aim-aim syndrome'. You must be willing to fire." – George S. Patton*

Doing the Right Thing, Visibly and Unwavering... Because

When you're leading, people are watching. They're watching what you do and how you do it, in all things. They will also form opinions about who you are and will ultimately decide if you're a person they can follow.

From the moment you arrive in a position of leadership, every action conveys meaning because it has a perceived or real impact on the team. Every thought that is said out loud, every name that is publicly forgotten, any flippant remark or sarcastic comment will be interpreted as having an underlying meaning.

Consistency is one of the most important characteristics of a strong leader. Saying what you mean and meaning what you say is the idea of making decisions regardless of circumstances. In good times and bad times, a good leader will provide a sense of certainty and direction that is needed. Be consistent in what you say and do. You can't show compassion one moment and pound your fist the next. The people around you need you to be predictable. Team members can't feel safe if they don't know what to expect from you.

Take a look at the way you're executing your leadership activities. Are you constantly living out your values? If you are, it will empower the environment and create significant moments of engagement. If you don't, you are (in effect) causing people to disengage and avoid you. As your leadership becomes bigger and has more power, whether it's perceived or real power, the scrutiny on you will grow.

Coaching Corner (Coach Tim)

Think for a moment about the message that's conveyed by being the first to arrive and the last to leave. It demonstrates acceptance, responsibility, accountability and ownership.

The people around you, specifically those you lead, are watching and making their own judgements from nearly every action you take. Own how you're showing up and do the things that ignite the best in others, not shut them down.

Remember: when no one is watching, everyone is… always.

> *"Every time you have to speak, you are auditioning for leadership." - James Humes*

Valuing Your Time…and the Time of Others

One of the words you probably don't expect to hear from your coach is an encouragement to be selfish. But that is indeed what you're going to hear from us. Be selfish with your time because it's the most valuable thing in the world.

When you become selfish with your time, put yourself first and then get your priorities in order, you will invariably maximize your results, relationships and impact. You will then have more energy, passion, and wisdom to give freely to others. But this only happens when you're selfish about where you spend your time.

On the other side of the issue is how you honor the time of others. We're constantly watching for behaviors and attitudes that create frustration and disengagement in the workplace. One of the ones that shows up the most is the disrespect of time.

Honestly, how you manage time, and the time of others, is a foundational statement of respect. Unfortunately for many leaders, they simply don't pay enough attention to this one simple, but profound, piece of the leadership puzzle.

How much are your words and actions showing how you value the 10,080 minutes you are given each week? If you're looking to move toward becoming a successful leader, assess how you spend your time. Ask yourself, "Is what I'm doing now, or what I'm going to do next, progressing our mission and important goals?" If it's not, it's time to recalibrate and get back to what is a priority.

The idea of "time" can vary greatly from individual to individual. As a leader, it's important for those you lead to understand where you stand on the value of time. What do you believe, expect, and consistently live out?

Other than behavior that is openly offensive, the misuse or disrespect of other people's time can be one of the strongest reasons for dissatisfaction in a leader. This includes being late, not showing up for scheduled meetings, multi-tasking rather than being present while speaking with others, holding meetings without agendas or exceeding the scheduled time limits due to disorganization. All of these send subtle and yet powerful messages about how you perceive the value of the time.

There are many resources available to you when it comes to productivity and time management, so we won't be going into great depths here. However, we're trying to paint the picture that it's the small things, like how you value and manage time, that can have a huge impact on your acceptance as a leader.

Successful leaders establish norms for scheduling team time and impacting the time of others. How time is aligned speaks to the extent to how much it truly is valued. As an aspiring leader, the message that you will want to consistently send is that your time, and the time of others, is deeply respected.

Prioritizing your time, and encouraging others to do the same, should have a deliberate purpose: it should boost your attitude, advance your health and relationships, and ignite growth. When your head hits the pillow each night, you should feel satisfied that you've invested in areas you care about and honor the things others care about as well.

"To add value to others, one must first value others." -- John Maxwell

Coaching Corner (Coach Chris)

If the majority of your leadership time isn't focused on your team, it's time for you to reevaluate. We encourage you to deploy these three "time rules" for effective leaders.

- **Make Time to Listen** - Build in weekly time for one-on-ones and huddles with your team. They can be a huge value-add, short touchpoint with your team members to keep everyone heading in the right direction and engaged along the way.

- **Make Time to Reflect** - Great leaders figure out ways to build in time for thought and reflection, both for themselves and for their team. Reflection allows you to think about what's going well and what course changes need to happen, assess growth, progress, and much more. It allows people to step outside of their day-to-day work and look at the larger strategy.

- **Make Time to Develop – In case you haven't heard**, annual performance reviews are dead. In their place, we want to build and sustain a coaching culture. Team members have made it widely known that they want more timely feedback and an ongoing growth and development plan. In other words, they want your help. Effective leadership involves setting up scheduled time to work with team members individually on their growth.

Transformation - Seeing the Opportunity Inside the Task

"I just want to be done."
"I wish we were finished with this project."
"How much longer do we need to do this?"

These could be the words of a nine-year-old child, a group of high school science classmates, or it could be the words of co-workers who just want the weekend to arrive. Whatever the case, if you were listening intently, you would hear loss or complaint in these words.

These examples speak to tasks being seen only as check boxes, not as opportunities for growth.

We call this being "stuck in a world of transactions". In this reality, it's all about getting things done. As a result, we miss the opportunity for transformation; not taking advantage of the learnings and growth that a task or experience could provide.

Inside each of these comments are opportunities for curiosity and creativity, innovation and problem solving, efficiency and effectiveness, modification and adaptability, and simple attitude adjustments and personal improvement. They're missed opportunities. They are the opportunities embedded in the work to examine options for changing a tedious task into a growth opportunity.

Our challenge to you: embrace the opportunity every task can provide. Move away from being stuck in "transaction mode" and find ways to make every task transformational. Change the story rattling through your mind from "woe" to "wow" when it matters most. The story you tell yourself about any situation is about 1% fact, and 99% interpretation. You completely control the interpretation side of it, so find a way to use it to your advantage.

Let's say you're going grocery shopping and you have your shopping list of things to get. Now, the typical way we tackle this would be to go to the store, pick up the items, come home and then you're finished. It's all about results and getting those transactions completed. You did it. Congrats.

The next time you go shopping, let's put a twist on it and challenge yourself to making this task 'transformational'. Play your cards this way:

- Before you head out, double check with your significant other to see if anything has changed (go beyond the initial request).
- When you get to the store and see an elderly person struggling to lift their groceries into their car, stop and assist. Greet them with sincerity and ask if you can assist. Guess what, no one else will know you did it. It's just the right thing to do. You're rarely in that much of a hurry that you can't stop for a moment and help someone, and it will probably make that person's day. (Find opportunities to serve.)
- Shop and be attentive to your surroundings. Make eye contact. (Be a human.)
- When you're at the checkout and the cashier asks how your day is, don't allow yourself to just respond with "fine", (a swear word in my home). Respond with a higher degree of being present and in return sincerely ask how the cashier's day is going. By the way, they will probably be stunned that you asked and may look at you funny. (Be present and authentic.)

Guess what? You just busted through the transactional barrier to a world of transformation. It's about grabbing the small things and helping each task be a "difference maker" in your world and the relationships around you.

Challenging yourself to see each activity as an opportunity to move from a compliance exercise to an opportunity for growth. Framing each interaction as an opportunity for motivation, support, and service. You'll get your tasks done, but through the art of transformation.

> *"Management is doing things right; leadership is doing the right thing." - Peter F. Drucker*

Are You Using the Right Tools?

In the game of leading, you're going to run into challenges and difficulties. As a result, one of the skills we must embrace is the capability to look at things from different perspectives and through numerous filters. Developing this discipline will position you to see solutions that may not have been considered in the past.

Albert Einstein believed that the effectiveness of an eventual solution resided in the depth of the consideration you give to the challenge being faced. Einstein went on to say, *"If I had an hour to solve a problem, I'd spend 55 minutes thinking about the problem and five minutes thinking about solutions."*

In our work with leaders about workplace culture, the area of "system and processes" is referred to as "Our Way". It's about looking at the tools we put in place to help get the job done. A responsibility that will eventually fall directly on your shoulders, if it hasn't already. We will dive deeper into this in our fourth book, the **Culture Champion**.

Let's just say that this an area where there is much angst in organizations. As you continue on your leadership quest, it becomes imperative that you look at systems and processes (the toolbox) that you have at your disposal with a critical eye.

You might be asking yourself what the issue of our "Our Way" has to do with your personal leadership journey. Along this quest, your comfort and willingness to leverage budgets, equipment, schedules, facilities, technology and most of all, people, is fundamental for being able to lead well.

As you reflect on this, we raise the question: are you trying to get the screw in with a hammer? Are you and your team fully leveraging the organizational assets in order to get the job done? Or is it time to look at the problems you're facing with new eyes, and potentially, new solutions.

Along your leadership quest, we encourage you to develop and leverage every tool in your toolbox for success. If something is missing, build it. If something is not working, fix it. Stop using the hammer if the job requires a screwdriver.

"Quality is not an act, it is a habit." - Aristotle

Coaching Corner (Coach Chris)

My wife and I live in a house built in 1910. As you hear that, I am sure you have some pictures that begin to form in your mind. The house has been an amazing place to raise our four children. Other people's kids might have a different perspective than mine. One point of contention is that our house only has one bathroom. Just ask our now-adult children about that experience. The stories are fascinating, entertaining and transformational!

We would not have been successful raising four kids in this home without designing and committing to strong systems and processes. This included schedules, budgets, room locations, weekly chore assignments, family values development, communication and feedback. For me, the real success in the story comes from working through it all.

We went from having a house to actually having a home, both in structure and in relationships.

Relentless Follow-Through

What are your "non-negotiables"? We could spend a ton of time working through your answer, but simply put, a "non-negotiable" is something you're unwavering on, no matter the circumstances. And if it's not already on your list, we have a non-negotiable we believe should be: the "relentless commitment to follow through".

Have you ever received this type of response from someone? *"I saw you called, but just forgot about it... sorry."* There simply is no place for this in the business world.

As a leader it's extremely important that you work diligently on "how" you choose to get the job done. This includes the values we aspire too, the attitudes we bring with us, and the actions we do, or do not, take.

Relentless follow-through represents your commitments. A commitment to the agreements that you make with others. As a leader, there is no room to compromise on your follow-through. It shows that you're a person who can't keep their promises, can't be trusted and someone who is not accountable. This will be a derailment to your leadership journey.

Leaders get work done. They see the challenges and problems in the work, and they figure out a way to move past/through them in order to achieve a goal. They exhibit a deep commitment to relentless follow-through.

Coaching Corner (Coach Tim)

What is the level of your 'stick-to-it-ness'?

The definition of resilience is: "someone who is able to withstand or recover quickly from difficult conditions or situations." As a leader, it's important to find your 'stick-to-it-ness', in other words: your ability to be resilient.

Being a resilient leader requires us to understand the changes happening in our environment, in our relationships, and in our responsibilities. It implies that difficulties, or unanticipated surprises, will be met with resolve. At its very core, resiliency means providing yourself and others around you with the assurance that whatever difficulties show up, we will work through them and be successful.

"Example is not the main thing in influencing others, it is the only thing." - Albert Schweitzer

CHAPTER 6:
The Price of Leadership

"We either make ourselves miserable or we make ourselves strong. The amount of work is the same."
– Carlos Castenada

When people first become aware of the influence that leaders can have, it quickly becomes an aspirational goal for many. There are very visible parts of the leadership role which appear very attractive and enticing to the casual observer. Being a leader means you have the authority to compel others to do your bidding, the ability to create and manage your own schedule, and the trappings of additional compensation.

The respect and adulation that successful leaders receive are just some of the alluring pieces which might prompt one to seek a leadership role. In reality, there is a price to be paid when you assume a position of leadership.

But along the way, we quickly realize there is a price to taking on leadership.

We all start our career journeys on the lower end of the totem pole. But there are many advantages on that end of things. You have the company of peers, the comradery of the team, the opportunity to converse and commiserate, and you often get insulation from responsibility. As we get promoted, things quickly change. The loss of these support mechanisms can cause the unprepared leader to quickly flounder.

The New Norm

Taking on a leadership role is categorically different than anything you've experienced before. The nature of every relationship will change. You're no longer just a team member; in fact, you've taken on responsibility and ultimate authority for the support, health, well-being and success of the team. It becomes more of a parental friendship than a collegial one.

Being the leader carries with it new and often not stated expectations. But it can also bring unexpected and often *unwanted* aspects.

Here are some examples:

People Expect You to Remember

As a leader, forgetting someone's birthday carries a set of assumptions and inferences that simply would not have occurred prior to assuming the role. Remembering birthdays, names of children, and important life circumstances is a leadership requirement.

Things Get Quiet When You Arrive

You need to prepare yourself for the first time that you enter the break room, and the conversation halts. You have to be prepared, metaphorically, to arrive at the party and hear the proverbial record scratch and have all of the voices go silent. While you may wish for the familiarity of the peer group, that time has passed.

Prepare to be Misunderstood

We begin to feel that during every interaction/conversation, no matter how personal and genuine it might feel in the moment, will end with some sort of a request. When this happens repeatedly, it can feel (to the leader) that they are being used for their position and influence.

Here Comes the Free Advice

Let's not forget about the endless supply of advice and suggestions you'll receive in preparation for an upcoming decision. Many of the thoughts you receive will appear informal and be proposed as helpful. However, when it comes time to make the hard decisions, there may well be many spectators and commentators, but the burden will reside squarely on you.

There is Always a Score

People, however well-intentioned they may be, keep score. There is no easy way to make everyone happy. In fact, sometimes you end making decisions that displease everyone.

Coaching Corner (Coach Tim)

The authority to make decisions doesn't exempt a leader from the need to be inclusive and thoughtful with regard to the participation of team members in the process. The practice of gathering additional input, even if the decision appears very clear, will serve to reinforce the strength of the team and position the leader well for future undertakings.

In many cases, the discipline of including thoughtful and skilled people in the process will surface suggestions that may well improve and enhance the ultimate decision.

Publicly showing appreciation for dissenting opinions can help. Taking time to share the rationale for the decisions and how differing positions were considered, can be seen as inclusionary. Ignoring the dynamic of perceived winners and losers as a result of the leader's decisions will quickly place the leader into a situation where 'factions' and conflicts can form. These factions ultimately inhibit the influence of the leader, and further create the feeling of isolation.

"Never confuse a single defeat with a final defeat." – F. Scott Fitzgerald

The Loneliness is Real

A distinct sense of isolation is arguably the most challenging change you will experience along your leadership quest. It speaks to the pressure and responsibility of leadership. Your new title is changing things.

Through the years, we've heard many leaders processing the changing relational dynamics. Casual actions or spoken words suddenly become fodder for second-guessing and ridicule. You soon come to the understanding that every step and every action must be preceded by a thoughtful consideration of how it will be perceived by others.

Besides the significant impact on working relationships, the additional reason for feeling particularly alone or isolated is that decisions ultimately rest on the shoulders of one individual: you. Our mistakes will be public and visible. Questions posed can often feel like challenges to our authority.

As you carry the mantle of leadership, you need be prepared for many interactions which appear to be socially and personally engaging, but they somehow seem to come around to a request. Your role as a leader places you in a position of influence and people are always looking for an opportunity to have you exert that influence on their behalf. It can be very disconcerting to realize that people (who you consider your friends) are now leveraging their relationship with you for their own personal benefit.

Being aware of the interactions you will experience and the reactions you will face after making tough decisions is a preparation that most aspiring leaders do not make. Knowing and preparing for the changes in relationships and interactions from former peers can help to lessen the feelings of isolation that leaders regularly experience.

> *"Character cannot be developed in ease and quiet. Only through experience of trial and suffering can the soul be strengthened, ambition inspired, and success achieved." – Helen Keller*

Looking Ahead

In the leadership role, you become charged with several levels of advanced planning and delivery. Near-term activities, which take place 30, 60 or perhaps 90 days into the future, are the focus of conversations that you will have most often with the team.

This focus by the team on the near-term activities and their completion is a reality that the leader must be able to support and encourage them on. It will reside, in contrast, to the intermediate planning of 6, 9, or 12 months, as well as the 3, 5 or 7-year long-term planning that leaders are called on to undertake.

Looking ahead, planning for the future, and making the necessary adjustments to the immediate course, so that long-term success can be ensured, will place you as the leader in a position that very few people on the team will genuinely understand. It will be that feeling of separation from those you lead.

Helping the team "connect the dots" between the activities of today and the intermediate and long-term planning is a necessity. Yet, the inertia of the daily demand on team members will create a situation where the overwhelming majority of responsibility for the long-term success will reside with you. It's up to you to chart the course, continue to look ahead and stay true to the course you have set, regardless of what other people think or the demands being placed on the work today.

The Committed Leader

One of our favorite books for leadership is *The Richest Man in Babylon* by George S. Clason. In the book, Clason explores the topics of thrift and the building of wealth. But as he does, he also conveys many messages about the importance of the "leading of self".

As we've discussed throughout this book, commitment to leading yourself well through purposeful self-discipline is known to be a cornerstone of success. The message of a commitment to a set of core values, the daily demonstration of self-respect, respect for others and the value of hard work are all points that the author makes through the use of stories set in ancient times. The lessons, however, are as applicable to aspiring leaders today as they were thousands of years ago.

When beginning a journey toward leadership, having a few key resources is very helpful. Clason's masterpiece on the building of personal wealth is so simple in its format that it's possible to miss the profound lessons the book holds. Carefully contained within this collection of parables are well crafted lessons that support the concept of "leading self" and being a positive example for the people we lead and work with.

Overcoming misfortune, finding ways forward when the path seems overwhelming, and achieving goals which seem out of reach. These are the themes that are brought into focus and explored.

> *"Opportunity is missed by most people because it's dressed in overalls and looks like work." – Unknown*

During your leadership quest, you will literally move from story to story. You'll be testing yourself to examine your own beliefs and assumptions about things obtained quickly and easily versus things that have lasting value because of the hard work and commitment that it took to attain.

Coaching Corner (Coach Chris & Tim)

As part of our own personal development, both of us love to read. We constantly read multiple books, take notes on and soak things in. As we'll talk about shortly, we both love the book "The Richest Man in Babylon". We encourage you to find time to pick up this great read for yourself. It'll be well worth your time!

But if we haven't convinced you yet to grab *The Richest Man in Babylon*, stop by our website and scan our book review.

We encourage you to drop by our website (www.firedupculture.com/readingroom) each month. We review a book we believe will inspire and equip you as a leader. Make sure you check it out!

"Leadership is a potent combination of strategy and character. But if you must be without one, be without the strategy." - Norman Schwarzkopf

Creating Margin and the Art of Setting Boundaries

Your people deserve a leader who demonstrates balance and the ability to manage your work-life balance, or what we refer to as the "margin in your life". With your leadership position comes the responsibility to model healthy lifestyle choices, including a life outside of the office.

I don't know about you, but I appreciate a good nap. Even twenty minutes of quiet rest and closing the eye lids. But this then changes when we become 'adults' and 'professionals'. As babies, we need naps and the world around us ensures we take them, for our health and the health of those around us. Then something happens. As adults, we're expected to 'suck it up' and get things done.

We want to chat with you about margin in your life. In our work worlds, we often speak about work-life balance, but the reality is that such a balance is not really achievable. As coaches, we encourage our clients to strive for margin, not balance.

You may now be asking yourself, "What is margin?" By our definition, margin is the gap between your current demands (and pace) compared to your limits or capacity.

Imagine for a moment a truck pulling a trailer. The trailer has a load limit. As you fill that trailer with items, the weight of the pull gets more challenging. However, if you load too much on that trailer, disaster will be just around the next corner. Combine a full load (capacity) with speed (pace) and serious consequences can show up in an instance.

That's the bad side of margin that we all experience. We simply have no room to move or respond. It's that feeling of having lots to do, and no time to do it. More importantly, you really feel the lack of margin as a leader when you need it the most. Your unavailable and unable to be responsive to the important relationships in your life.

Remember: as leaders, we're in the relationship game. If you're unavailable and unable to be responsive to the important relationships in your life, what has really been achieved?

A lack of margin is truly the enemy of your leadership journey. But it's not the heavy load that breaks you down. It's the way you carry it.

You really have three choices when it comes to margin in your life, both personally and professionally:

Choice #1 - Live *below* your limits
Choice #2 - Live *at* your limits
Choice #3 - Live *above* your limits

Which choice do you think you should strive for as a leader? If you answered, "below your limits", you're correct. However, the reality for most of us, either new to leadership or seasoned, is that we're constantly "at" or "above" our limits because of the demands being placed on us.

Let us paint a quick picture for you. Imagine you have a balloon in your hands and you're getting ready to blow it up. As you do, you know that feeling of it getting really full? It's quickly approaching the 'burst' zone. That's the balloon's capacity and you've just filled it with a load of air that is testing its limits.

When it comes to margin and boundaries in your life, you don't want to fill your 'balloon' until it's full. It can only hold so much. Set boundaries and respect them.

So, what can you do to ensure that you have good margins in your life? Get really good at setting and holding true to your boundaries.

The art of setting boundaries is difficult and requires courage.

Brené Brown is a New York Times best-selling author, lecturer and podcaster focused on self-empowerment, courage and empathy. Brown said it best when she stated: "Daring to set boundaries is about having the courage to love ourselves, even when we risk disappointing others. We can't base our own worthiness on others' approval. Only when we believe, deep down, that we are enough, can we say, enough!"

Here is a simple rule that we would encourage you to follow. Every time you say "yes" to something, it's essential to also find something you can say "no" to. The unmanageable workload is one of the most impactful factors for causing burnout. So, your ability to set boundaries and protect them is a critical skill that could mean the difference between a successful journey and one of failure.

As you truly grasp and deploy the art of setting boundaries in your world, keep a few specifics in mind.

Firstly, know your limits. Each of us is different. This includes our energy levels, our ability to focus, our values and priorities. Know who you are, what's important to you and then make decisions accordingly. You're not living anyone else's script or playing someone else's music. Know your limits and protect them.

Secondly, pay attention to your feelings. Let's refer this back into the 'nap time' point we talked about earlier. I'm sure we all know that feeling when it's time to take a nap. If you need one, or you need to take some space, do it. Don't wait for others to have to tell you. Don't find yourself ignoring your feelings or pushing them down. It doesn't work. Feelings and emotions will eventually get the better of you and the pain in the end will be greater than anything you may experience today.

Finally, give yourself permission. Permission to own who you are. Permission to create structure and boundaries in your world. Permission to say "no". Permission to pause before saying "yes". Permission to take time off and invest in yourself. You're worth it, and the world deserves the best version of you at all times.

As the author, Henry Cloud, wrote in his book *Boundaries for Leaders*: "The problem is that sometimes you see boundaries as an offensive weapon. Nothing could be further from the truth. Boundaries are a defensive tool. Appropriate boundaries don't control, attack, or hurt anyone. They simply prevent your treasures from being taken at the wrong time."

You need to set your own boundaries; the world won't do it for you.

> *"You can only become truly accomplished at something you love. Don't make money your goal. Instead, pursue the things you love doing, and then do them so well that people can't take their eyes off you." -Maya Angelou*

Coaching Corner (Coach Chris)

One of the tools for getting to a solid "YES" and a solid "NO" for things in your life is to deploy a strategy of diverting, withdrawing, quitting and abandoning. You probably never imaging hearing those words from a coach! Let me explain.

- **Divert Daily** – Divert things daily that are creating distractions or are not a priority. Stay focused on what <u>is</u> important.

- **Withdrawal Weekly** – Find your rhythm for pulling back, catching your breath and taking space.

- **Quit Quarterly** – Look for things that you can 'quit' i.e., stop doing, each quarter. Find the one thing that you can ditch to create space for the things that you want to do instead.

- **Abandon Annually** – Every year, carve out some space as you set out plans for your future. During this time, move away from activities, behaviors and people that are not helping you to achieve your goals.

CHAPTER 7:
Final Thoughts

"Do not stop thinking of life as an adventure. You have no security unless you can live bravely, excitingly, imaginatively."
- Eleanor Roosevelt

Life can sometimes be overly complicated. It's hard to make sense of everything that's happening around us. This is particularly true as you tackle the journey of leadership.

As coaches, we thrive on taking the complex and making it more manageable. It's our hope that you've found many personal and meaningful nuggets along your quest through this book and that it has encouraged you to continue along the journey toward successful leadership.

Today's business climate places great demands on leadership. As a leader, you're expected to meet all the expectations of your stakeholders, increase productivity, create great relations with team members and customers. You're also expected to foresee any impending challenges and be an architect of a workplace that will attract and retain top talent.

Our ultimate job as leaders is to create a highly engaging workplace culture. A place where people voluntarily raise their hands and say, "I want to be part of that." Yes, there may be a paycheck or two passed from the organization to the individual, but that is simply a transaction.

We want to create a place where people *choose* to use their talents and unique strengths for doing good, achieving impact and getting transformational results. Work becomes lighter and more rewarding when we're in a community.

Amazing workplaces and transformational impact all boil down to leadership. This is where you come in. Start today from wherever you find yourself along the leadership journey. Your quest will lead to many unseen nor unanticipated things. Be courageous.

By putting a few of the nuggets you've discovered in this book into practice, we believe you will experience personal growth, amazing relationships and tremendous impact. Whatever you dream of today is only the start. It's just a beginning.

We are firm believers in you. We are your champions, and we look forward to hearing how your leadership quest, and all the stories it will contain, will unfold.

Thank you for spending a few moments of your time with us through the pages of this book.

We look forward to continuing the conversation.
Get Up. Show Up. Fire Up. Own It. Lead On!

Additional Resources

We view the 'quest' toward leadership as a first step. Leading yourself well is a lifelong journey, full of daily decisions, attitude check-ins, conversations, failures and growth.

If you would like to dive deeper into the journey of forming life-giving relationships, building amazing teams and becoming a culture champion, we recommend the resources here as a next step in the journey.

For continually updated resources, visit *www.wouldyouworkforyou.com* or *www.firedupculture.com*. Additionally, you can continue the conversation with us on LinkedIn or Twitter. We invite you to connect with us directly: @chrisihrig or @yeomats

Book References

Fired Up Brands is deeply dedicated to building exceptional resources to assist you, your team and your organization. As part of the ***Would You Work for You Series***, the additional books are available from a variety of resources, including our websites (above) and on Amazon.

As a current friend of the firm, you can receive the best prices and personal service by simply visiting *www.wouldyouworkforyou.com*. Whether you're looking for one book or purchasing in bulk for your team, our specialized care team are on hand to help you.

As a special limited time offer, use the code **WYWFY15** for a 15% discount on your next order.

About the Authors – Chris

> *"People who are crazy enough to think they can change the world, are the ones who do..." – Rob Siltanen*

 Chris J. Ihrig was born and raised in Seattle, Washington. He attained a BA from The Evergreen State College and an MBA in Organizational Development from Regent University. After that, he went on to work in a variety of roles in corporate leadership.

He currently lives in the Pacific Northwest with his wife of 33 years, Kris, and their dog, Lilly. He and his wife are very proud parents of four adult children and their growing extended family.

In his free time, Chris enjoys playing golf, watching baseball as well as studying history and technology. His great passion is his 1982 Jaguar XJS and he enjoys driving it every time he gets behind the wheel. When he gets the chance, he enjoys traveling, immersing himself in different cultures, connecting with people and nature, and sampling food from around the world.

Chris has been recognized nationally as an authority in the fields of Leadership Development, Organizational Change and Culture. He is passionate and thankful for the opportunity to serve his community, having recently completed a ten-year stint as an elected School Board Member. Chris particularly enjoys supporting programs and professionals who impact the lives of those with disabilities and special needs.

As far as his future vision is concerned, Chris wants to continue building a high-impact organization with significant reach, write more books, travel more and become a master golfer.

You can contact Chris on:

LinkedIn: *https://www.linkedin.com/in/chrisihrig/*

Twitter: *@chrisihrig*

Email: *cihrig@firedupculture.com*

About the Authors – Tim

> *"Strive not to be a success, but rather to*
> *be of value..." – Albert Einstein*

Dr. Timothy (Tim) Yeomans hails from Seattle, Washington. In his youth, he spent a lot of time with his grandparents on Vashon Island, where he developed his yet undiminished love for the outdoors.

He currently resides in Southern Oregon with his wife and their dogs and enjoys partaking in the wonderful weather and natural beauty that the area affords.

With an education that spans several fields, including European History, German, Education, Policy Studies and Leadership, Tim holds bachelor's and master's degrees from Washington State University and a Doctorate from the University of Washington.

He currently serves as an Organizational Leadership Consultant and Executive Coach, following over a decade of leading school systems in the Washington area. He has also worked for many years as a university lecturer and an adjunct professor in the field of Education Leadership.

In his free time, Tim enjoys walking his dogs along the Oregon coastline with his wife, Erin, spending time with family and friends, overlooking the vineyards of the Umpqua Valley and exploring the backroads of North America.

He has been recognized nationally for his leadership and service in the field of Education Leadership and in the Puget Sound region for his work on racial equity and broadening educational opportunities for underserved populations.

You can contact Tim on:

LinkedIn: *www.linkedin.com/in/timothy-yeomans-6334963a/*

Twitter: *@yeomats*

Email: *tyeomans@firedupculture.com*

About Our Firm – Fired Up Culture

Fired-Up! Culture is a business management and human resource consulting firm with corporate headquarters in the Pacific Northwest. Over the past few decades, our team has partnered with organizations and leaders around the globe to build business cultures that engage people and achieve breakthrough results.

Fired-Up! Culture's mission is to equip and build leadership capacity through talent management-focused consulting services that provide relevant and timely resources for our clients. Fired-Up's commitment to excellence supports a focused and intentional investment in the people and systems of these organizations to achieve breakthrough results.

Our leadership development and change management processes are used by a diverse client base around the world. We've had the privilege of shaping the philosophies, practices and skills of thousands of dynamic leaders, managers and teams. Our tools have been successfully used and implemented by hundreds of organizations and their team members.

Our coaching, consulting and facilitation services provide the focus and insight needed to drive lasting change.

For more information about Fired Up!, please visit:
Website: *www.firedupculture.com*
Twitter: *@firedupculture*

Made in the USA
Monee, IL
19 June 2021